Researchers have found that if you meditate twenty minutes a day for eight weeks, there will be a measurable changes in your brain waves. Hopefully, for the better, right? You probably won't be able to sit comfortably in a snow bank in your underwear or levitate during your meditation. Too bad about that. But you'll be more relaxed and focused and less likely to become upset over small things.

Studies have found that meditation can lower blood pressure, slow the progression of HIV, relieves pain, and helps with chronic diseases like allergies, and arthritis. Meditation also helps resolve phobias and fears, leads to deeper levels of relaxation and decreases muscular tension.

Meditation provides peace of mind and allows you to keep everything in perspective. You learn to forgive yourself and others and increase your sense of compassion. You achieve a deeper understanding of yourself and others and that leads to greater wisdom, and opportunities to find direction and focus in your life. Through meditation you can achieve what you aspire. Think of life as gain, not pain.

Copyright © 2015 by RobMacGregor
Cover illustration by Dave Dodd
Design by Aaron Rosenberg
ISBN 978-1-941408-37-7 — ISBN 978-1-941408-38-4 (pbk.)
All rights reserved. No part of this book may be used or reproduced in any manner whatsoever without written permission except in the case of brief quotations embodied in critical articles and reviews.
Panta Rei Press is an imprint of Crossroad Press Publishing
For information address Crossroad Press at 141 Brayden Dr., Hertford, NC 27944
www.crossroadpress.com

First edition

JEWEL IN THE LOTUS

Rob MacGregor

Contents

Introduction

PART ONE—FINDING THE JEWEL
  Chapter 1: Getting Started
  Chapter 2: Relaxation
  Chapter 3: Mindfulness
  Chapter 4: Breathe
  Chapter 5: Mantras & Chants
  Chapter 6: Affirmations
  Chapter 7: Visualization
  Chapter 8: Inquiry
  Chapter 9: Chakras

PART TWO—EXPLORING THE JEWEL
  Chapter 10: Directed Meditations
      Abundance
      Breaking Blockages
      Finding Your Path in Life
      Meeting Your Soul Mate
      Self-Healing
      Intuitive Guidance
      Overcoming Negativity
      Enhancing Creativity
  Chapter 11: PSI & the Siddhi
  Chapter 12: Ease & Disease

PART THREE—JOURNEYS WITH THE JEWEL
  Chapter 13: Shamanic Meditation
      The Lower World
      The Upper World
      The Middle World

PART FOUR—BEYOND THE JEWEL
  Chapter 14: Meditation as Activism

Introduction

"Meditation takes us from survival to creation; from separation to connection; from imbalance to balance; from emergency mode to growth —and-repair mode; and from the limiting emotions of fear, anger, and sadness to the expansive emotions of joy, freedom, and love. Basically, we go from clinging to the known to embracing the unknown."
—Dr. Joe Dispenza, *You are the Placebo: Making Your Mind Matter*

Om Mani Padme Hum.
 Go ahead. Say it aloud. It's a Sanskrit chant. It won't hurt, but it might help.

Good. Now that everyone reading this page has heard *Om Mani Padme Hum* at least once, we're moving in the right direction. But what does it mean?

The literal translation of the chant is *The Jewel in the Lotus*. Yes, the title of this book.

Now that you know what the chant means in English, you're probably *still* wondering, 'What does it mean?' After all, why would anyone go around chanting *The Jewel in the Lotus...The Jewel in the Lotus...The Jewel in the Lotus.*

Let's take a closer look at *Om Mani Padme Hum*.

Om is said to be the sound of the universe at creation. People chant Om to resonate with the universe. *Mani* means jewel. *Padme* means lotus. *Hum* is the sound of triumph when we all wake up and recognize our true selves, that we are more than what we seem. In other words, enlightenment.

You could call this chant the Big Bang of self-development. It's about transformation to a higher state of being. A friend, Jeri, who has an import business and travels to Nepal once a year on a buying trips, hears this chant everyday, morning and night. People chant it in temples and their homes. Some people walk down a city street or a rural path chanting it. They're Buddhists, but you don't have to be one to chant. (Buddhism actually is more of a philosophy than a religion and accepts the truths of all religions.)

So Jeri has thought about this chant, this mantra, this prayer, and she described it in a very lyrical way when I asked her what she thought it meant. "The jewel within the lotus represents the mystery of life. It's the budding complexity within which dwells the jewel of truth. It's a prayer for others as well as for oneself. It is a prayer for all sentient beings to become enlightened. As consciousness is raised throughout the world, the benefit to all of us is realized."

Nice. It's a mantra that contains potential. In fact, it's said that *all* the teachings of the Buddha are contained in it. Think about that. It's like a seed that can become the Tree of Life. *Om Mani Padme Hum*. Say it again. Say it a few times. Shut the door if you don't want anyone to hear you chanting Sanskrit.

But you can also say it to yourself. Tibetan Buddhists believe that saying *Om Mani Padme Hum*, aloud or silently, or even just seeing it written on this page, invokes the powerful benevolent attention and blessings of Chenrezig. Now who's that, you might ask. Glad you did. Chenrezig is the Lord of Love, the embodiment of compassion. And who doesn't want some help from the Lord of Love?

So *Om Mani Padme Hum* is a call for blessings, for attaining whatever it is that you seek.

Now you have a better understanding of the title. But what can *you* expect to achieve through meditation? A lot.

Researchers have found that if you meditate twenty minutes a day for eight weeks, there will be a measurable changes in your brain waves. Hopefully, for the better, right? You probably won't be able to sit comfortably in a snow bank in your underwear or levitate during your meditation. Too bad about that. But you'll be more relaxed and focused and less likely to become upset over small things.

Part One covers the basics. By following the meditations, you'll soon be more centered and aware and more in control of your emotions. You'll also be able to quiet your busy mind—sometimes called the monkey mind! Sorry about that.

On another level, meditations can be directed toward particular goals, things you want in life. But wait, you might say, isn't meditation a spiritual practice? Isn't it about being detached from the everyday world and our desires? Good question. While meditation isn't exactly a trip to the candy store, it's not a journey to the god of dentistry, either.

It's about seeking higher awareness, happiness, and fulfillment. It's about finding peace and balance in our lives. And the best way to achieve those things is to ask for them. After all, essentially we are all spiritual beings experiencing a physical existence. We come from spirit and we return to spirit. Our job is to do the best we can with what we've got. In spirit, desires can be instantaneously manifested. In the physical world, we have to work harder at achieving what we want. But we need to remember that it all comes from within before it is manifested in the physical.

That's what directed meditations, the subject of Part 2 is all about that—manifesting from within.

But I'm getting ahead of myself. Let's first try to make sense of meditation. Why does it work?

Science & Meditation

Over the past sixty years, hundreds of studies have been conducted on the effects of meditation. One such study, involving Yale, Harvard and the Massachusetts General Hospital, found that meditation increases gray matter in specific regions of the brain and may slow the deterioration of the brain as a part of the natural aging process. In other words, meditation can reverse aging.

Another study found that meditation produced significant increases in left-sided anterior brain activity, which is associated with positive emotional states. So negative emotions are reduced; positive emotions are increased. As a result, meditation influences mood and behavior and increases emotional stability.

According to University of Wisconsin neuroscientist Richard Davidson, experienced meditators exhibit high levels of gamma wave activity and, as a result, have an ability to control their thoughts and their reactions to changing circumstances. Related benefits are increased creativity, improved learning ability and memory, focus and concentration. Meditation also builds self-confidence. All these things are linked to achieving your goals.

Meditators are more alert after meditation than non-meditators. In a 2006 study, college students were asked to sleep, watch TV, or meditate. They were then tested on their alertness by hitting a button whenever a light flashed on a screen. The meditators surpassed the sleepers and TV watchers by ten percent. That supports other studies that show that meditation enhances energy, strength and vigor.

Studies have found that meditation can lower blood pressure, slow the progression of HIV, relieves pain, and helps with chronic diseases like allergies, and arthritis. Meditation also helps resolve phobias and fears, leads to deeper levels of relaxation and decreases muscular tension.

Meditation provides peace of mind and allows you to keep everything in perspective. You learn to forgive yourself and others and increase your sense of compassion. You achieve a deeper understanding of yourself and others and that leads to greater wisdom, and opportunities to find direction and focus in your life. Through meditation you can achieve what you aspire. Think of life as gain, not pain.

My Background

So who am I to be telling you all of this stuff?

I've taught yoga for more than twenty years, in both gyms and yoga studios. I've been involved in a number of different styles over the years, starting my practice before the advent of sticky mats, when yoga students tended to wear loose, white cotton garb. Most of the studios were carpeted and we practiced on bath towels. Yeah, a long time ago.

I've had a variety of yoga teachers and meditation guides. As such, I'm not a practitioner of any one particular style of yoga or meditation. Most meditation practices are derived from Eastern philosophy and religion. But meditation is also part of Native America heritage, which we explore in Part 3. I've learned from each tradition and developed my own style of meditation, which I've taught in a yoga studio and fitness center in South Florida.

Of course I've done other things as well. That's one advantage of getting older. You've had more time to do stuff. In my 20s and early 30s, I worked as a journalist and editor, and then turned to full time freelance writing—both fiction and non-fiction. I'm probably best known in the writing world as the author of seven Indiana Jones novels, including the adaptation of *Indiana Jones and The Last Crusade*. I've also won the Edgar Allan Poe award for my young adult novel, *Prophecy Rock*, and was a finalist for the award for *Hawk Moon*.

In non-fiction, I wrote a yoga book called, *The Lotus & the Stars: The Way of Astro-Yoga* (Contemporary Books, 2001), a style that blends yoga and astrology. I also created a meditation CD that came with another book I wrote, *Psychic Power: Discover and Develop Your Sixth Sense at Any Age* (Barron's, 2005).

In this book, the focus is not only on learning to meditate, but applying it to your everyday life. Before we move on, let's say it one more time:

Om Mani Padme Hum.

PART ONE
FINDING THE JEWEL

Chapter 1

Getting Started

"If you want to conquer the anxiety of life, live in the moment, live in the breath."

— Amit Ray, *Om Chanting and Meditation*

My definition of meditation is a practice that allows us to connect to a deeper part of ourselves, our true self, and through this connection we can take more control of our lives, are more relaxed and focused, and can heal ourselves. It's about self-discovery, expanding our awareness, and achieving our goals.

However, you'll probably encounter some distractions on your journey inward. In fact, you might initially think that the *real* definition of meditation is a practice that involves a constant battle to quiet your mind. Yes, the mind is an unruly companion when you meditate. It tends to speak out of turn, keeping you from entering a deeper state of relaxation and meditation. But you can win this battle, ironically, by not considering it a battle. You'll see what I mean shortly. First, let's start with some basics.

Find your Place & Time

It's best to meditate in the same place and around the same time every day. Find a spot where you won't be disturbed, where you can return day after day at your meditation time and count on not being interrupted by matters from the everyday world. You'll have enough challenge to escape those matters in your mind without actually confronting them while you're trying to meditate.

I meditate on our back porch the first thing in the morning before I eat breakfast, before I turn on my computer, read or see the news or talk to anyone other than my meditation partner, a Golden Retriever named Noah. He knows when it's time to meditate and alerts me if I'm tardy. He'll stand at the door, waiting to get started. Dogs are pattern-oriented creatures and Noah knows that I sit and he lies down at my feet at a certain time and place. Of course, not all dogs will put up with a meditating master without a few disturbing nudges or yips for attention.

Finding your Position

Meditation doesn't require any particular posture. The traditional way is to sit cross-legged on a cushion on the floor. But if that's uncomfortable, don't let it stop you from meditating. You can sit on a chair with your feet on the floor. The idea is to get comfortable, but not so comfortable that you fall asleep. So if lying down is your best option, don't do it where you sleep. Otherwise, meditation might be a brief prequel to a nap.

My intent, of course, is for you to experience meditation, not just read about it. Besides, if you follow my instructions, you'll have a hard time reading with your eyes closed.

First Steps

So let's get right into it. Hopefully, you have some quiet time and a place where you won't be interrupted. If that's not the case, come back later and start with these introductory meditations.

Easy Entry

If you're meditating for the first time, think of it as a baby learning to walk. Toddlers wobble and fall, but get up and try again. Before long, walking becomes second nature. The same can be true for meditation—except you're not likely to fall down.

Assume a comfortable position. Stay attentive, but relaxed. Close your eyes and take two or three long, slow deep breaths. Just sit or lie down and let your mind do whatever it wants for no longer than five minutes. Don't worry about it. Don't force anything or question what you're doing. Just relax, but pay attention. Give yourself this time. Think of it as a reward. Open your eyes when you think enough time has elapsed.

M-E-D-I-T-A-T-E

If you followed my suggestion and took a few minutes to meditate—that's the idea here—hopefully it didn't feel like the longest five minutes of your life. Were you actually able to quiet your mind without much effort? If you were able to do so for more than a few short seconds, then you're a natural, or an experienced meditator.

What were you thinking about? Did your mind wander to the point that you forgot that you were attempting to meditate? Categorize your thoughts. Did your mind drift to the past, to something that happened earlier, to what you're going to do later? Were you worrying, questioning, planning, thinking about a conversation, fretting, going over your to-do list? How did you get there? See if you can trace your thoughts back. Notice how one thought led to another.

Now take another few minutes to resume your meditation. However, this time pay attention to your thoughts. Think of your thoughts as a flowing river and you are typically flowing in that river. With meditation, we swim to shore and sit on the bank and allow the river of thoughts to flow by. We realize that we are not our thoughts. We can find quiet outside that flowing river. We can observe the river without getting caught up in it.

Like I said, you don't have to battle the mind to win the battle. Stay with it a few minutes.

M-E-D-I-T-A-T-E

Mind Your Mind

Now that you've had a chance to dabble with meditation, let's get into the heart of the matter. We all understand the notion of getting physically fit through a work out in a gym or taking a yoga class, but we don't usually think about getting a mind workout through meditation. That's because we're too busy thinking and doing, and meditation is neither. Meditation has great value for improving our lives in a lot of ways—physiologically, psychologically, and spiritually—but the fact is our minds are usually busy planning for the future or remembering the past.

So how do we meditate? Simply put, meditation is about *relaxing and focusing*. That's not what meditation is, but it's the *process*, the method to achieve it. You'll know when you're there. You'll feel an inner calm, and as you go even deeper, you'll seemingly move outside of normal time and space. Your mind might travel on its own in a way that is not about thinking. Time flies. Forty minutes can pass so swiftly you might think you've experienced missing time.

So, is this stuff dangerous? What happens to our brains when we achieve such a deeply relaxed, meditative state? From a scientific point of view, our brain waves move into the alpha state. That's a level of consciousness between wakefulness and sleep. Research has shown that people who meditate regularly can move their brains easily into the alpha state.

That's a good thing, because it promotes healing and a sense of well-being. The alpha state also improves our concentration and focus, relieves stress, and promotes creativity. It's the state of mind we enter for directed meditations, where we focus on an intention that might be about a relationship, healing, abundance, or any number of other goals.

In addition to those advantages, we can move toward a higher state of consciousness, a place that exists outside of our everyday reality where we can commune with the non-physical, with deceased relatives and ancestors, with higher beings of light. All sorts of things can happen. That's part of the realm of shamanic meditation.

Relaxing and Focusing

You would think relaxation would be the easiest part of meditation. But that's not necessarily so. Our bodies can be tense after a day at the workplace or even before work when we're looking ahead to upcoming challenges. The next chapter will focus on deep relaxation.

The other major aspect of meditation—focusing—provides direction for the mind, to keep it from wandering. Easier said than done. There actually are three types of focusing:

mindfulness, focusing on a single word or phrase, watching your thoughts and staying in the present moment,

imaging or *visualization*, where you create images with your mind's eye, and usually have a goal in mind — such as healing yourself, and

inquiry, asking a question and watching for an answer through images or voices or other sensations. Think of it as a kind of conscious dreaming.

We'll take a close look at each of those triggers for meditation in coming chapters, but let's relax first. Really relax.

Meditation Joke #1

A student went to his meditation teacher and said, "My meditation is horrible! I feel so distracted, or my legs ache, or I'm constantly falling asleep. It's just horrible!"

"It will pass," the teacher said matter-of-factly.

A week later, the student came back to his teacher. "My meditation is wonderful! I feel so aware, so peaceful, so alive! It's just wonderful!"

"It will pass," the teacher replied matter-of-factly.

Chapter 2

Relaxation

"The sensation of energy expands with increasing relaxation."

—Ilchi Lee

'Hurry up and Relax'

Years ago, I had a yoga teacher who liked to begin his classes with a short session of relaxation. He was usually anxious to get started so he would say, "Okay, onto our backs. Let's hurry up and relax." He often got laughs from the comment, which seems like an oxymoron. After all, we tend to link 'hurry up' directives with stress, not relaxation.

Let's talk about stress. It's a good thing. At least in manageable doses. Stress relates to our survival instinct: our efforts to achieve our goals and protect ourselves. It's triggered when we face a threat or challenge. But when we are constantly on high alert, charged for action, prepared for any threats, stress becomes an addiction, a way of life. If we're not rushing around, doing and thinking, we feel bored and directionless, and worried that we're missing out on something.

However, when you're habitually operating under stress, you can become sick and unhappy as your body and emotions crash from chronic tension. Your breath is often shallow and rapid. Your sympathetic nervous system dominates and you repeatedly shift into a 'fight or flight' mode. You don't eat well. You don't fully digest your food, and you hold onto toxic emotions from the past. As a result, you don't heal physically or emotionally.

I recall meeting a friendly handyman, who was capable of fixing or repairing anything. When he found out I taught meditation classes, he shook his head and said he could never sit still for five minutes, much less an hour. He was busy and he liked it that way. Always something to do, rushing from one job to another. A few months later, I was told that he'd fallen off his ladder and died. I couldn't help thinking that he might still be alive if he'd slowed and taken more time to relax.

While stress serves as a mechanism that allows you to protect yourself and fight for survival, moving into a relaxed state enables you to lower your defenses and unwind. You open yourself to healing, expanded awareness, and happiness. But what does it mean to relax?

Some people equate relaxing with an alcoholic drink after work. For others, it's watching television or playing a computer game, listening to music or reading a novel. All those things probably help people take their minds off whatever makes them tense, anxious or upset. But the next day the scenario is repeated as the stress level builds again.

As you might've guessed, there's another way to relax, one that helps ease the daily stress, that moves body and mind into a comfort zone, a realm outside of the everyday world, free of worries.

You might protest: 'But I've got a lot to worry about, and I don't have time for any escapism.' That attitude, unfortunately, is what leads to more stressful circumstances and even illnesses. Ironically, relaxing and letting go of your everyday concerns helps you deal with stressful issues in a positive way.

If you've taken yoga classes, you're probably familiar with *savasana*. That's the relaxation pose, lying on your back, or as it's sometimes referred, the corpse pose. Clearly, the Sanskrit name sounds more appealing, even if you don't know what it means.

Some yoga teachers refer to savasana as the most important pose. I often call it a well-deserved resting pose at the end of my yoga classes. Interestingly, B.K.S. Iyengar, a renowned yoga teacher, the creator of Iyengar yoga, calls it one of the most difficult poses. Here's what he says in his book, *Light on Yoga*:

"....By remaining motionless for some time and keeping the mind still while fully conscious, you learn to relax. This conscious relaxation invigorates and refreshes both body and mind. But it is much harder to keep the mind than the body still. Therefore, this apparently easy yoga posture is one of the most difficult to master."

You've probably never thought of relaxing as difficult, but Iyengar makes a good point. Your body might be at ease while lying on your back, but turning off your active mind is another matter. That's the challenge we face when we move into the relaxation mode.

Progressive Muscle Relaxation

Here's a step-by-step method for moving into a deeply relaxed state, one that will prepare you for directed meditation, or simply help relieve stress. It won't take long to memorize the sequence, especially if you practice it a couple of times, referring to the text whenever you're uncertain about what follows.

Settle down in a place where you won't be disturbed. Lie down, but avoid turning to the position in which you usually sleep. Your intent is to move into a deeply relaxed state for fifteen to twenty minutes, while remaining awake.

First, take a few deep diaphragmatic breaths, rounding your belly with the inhalation, then letting the belly sink toward the spine on the exhalation. After at least three such breaths, shift to three-part yogic breathing. Start the same way by rounding your belly on the inhalation, then roll the bubble of air upward to the middle of your chest, sniff in a little more air, and roll the bubble to your upper chest. Exhale, releasing all the air, and repeat two or three times. Finally, shift to gentle breathing.

You're probably already starting to feel more relaxed, but we're just getting started. Ironically, one way to relax your body is by creating tension in the muscles, joints, ligaments and tendons. By tensing and relaxing body parts, you recognize the relaxed state through the contrast.

Begin with your feet. Curl your toes, tensing your feet, your calves, your thighs and the muscles in your buttocks. Now lift your heels a few inches. Hold for several seconds, then relax. Make tight fists with your hands, tense your shoulders and lift your arms a few inches. Hold several seconds, then let go.

Next, squeeze your shoulders up toward your ears, hold and release. Now arch your back, pushing your shoulder blades closer together, sliding your tailbone under you. Hold several seconds, then release. Lift your hips, hold, then let yourself down.

Lift your arms and legs, make fists, curl your toes, take a deep breath, hold it and squeeze all the muscles in your face toward your nose. Exhale, then release, noticing the difference between your tensed and relaxed muscles. Finally, roll into a ball with your thighs against your belly, arms wrapped around your shins, forehead toward your knees. Hold and release onto your back with your legs apart and palms turned up.

Take a couple more deep, diaphragmatic breaths. Then slow your breath. Next, turn your focus from your breath to your body. Starting with the crown of your head, and imagine invisible fingers massaging your scalp. Take your time. Enjoy the imaginary massage.

Now allow those invisible fingers to move onto your forehead and spread outward around your temples. The relaxing sensation moves around your eye sockets, over the bridge of your nose, along your cheekbones, and then down your jaw. Leave a gap between your teeth and let your tongue come down from the roof of your mouth. Relax all of your facial muscles.

The soothing energy flows over your neck, then your shoulders, your upper arms, your elbows and forearms. Let your wrists, hands and fingers relax. Let the palms of your hands relax.

Now the relaxation ripples over your chest and down your upper back, lower back, around your rib cage, and over your abdomen. Your hip bones relax in their sockets and your buttocks relax. Now the soothing sensation eases down over your thighs. Your kneecaps float on your knees. The backs of your knees relax. Your shins and calves relax. Your ankles, feet and toes relax. The bottoms of your feet relax.

As you continue gentle breathing, relax your circulatory system. Become aware of the beat of your heart and the flow of your blood through the arteries, capillaries, and back through the veins to the heart. Relax all of your internal organs and glands. Relax...relax... relax.

Relax your nervous system. You have six hundreds miles of tiny neurons running through body. There are more nerve cells in the human brain than stars in the Milky Way. Your brain alone contains, a universe unto itself!

Finally, relax your mind. Pay attention to your breath. Stay in the present moment. Notice how relaxed you feel. Remain still for as long as you like. Then open your eyes and lift up onto your forearms. Bend your knees and with your feet planted, swing your knees from side to side a few times. Then sit up.

Here's a variation you can try.

Scanning in Reverse

You can also scan your body in the opposite direction, starting with your feet and working upward. This time, rather than tensing and releasing all the muscles at the beginning of the session, you'll contract and release the muscles as you move slowly along the body.

Tensing and Releasing

Stretch out on your back in your place of meditation. Begin by taking several long, slow, deep breaths, then shift to gentle breathing. As you do so, bring your focus to your left foot. Curl your toes, tensing your foot…then release. Notice how your relaxed foot feels, including the toes and the bottom of the foot.

Next move to your lower left leg and notice how your calf feels. Tense your calf. Hold for a few seconds, then release. Turn your focus to your left thigh. Tense the thigh, then let it go. Now tense your left buttock… and release it.

Shift your attention to your right foot. Squeeze the toes together, tensing the foot several seconds, then release. Move your awareness to your lower right leg and tighten your calf. Let it go and notice how your relaxed calf feels. Next focus on your right thigh. Tense, hold, and release. Take your attention to your right buttock, tense it…then release.

Now contract the muscles of buttocks and lift your hips slightly. Hold several seconds, feeling the tension in the hips and pelvis, then relax the muscles as you settle back down.

Bring your attention to your abdominal muscles, tensing for a few seconds. Notice the tension in your lower back as well, then release and relax. Move your awareness to your chest, tensing it. At the same time, contract the muscles in your upper back, pushing your shoulder blades together. Hold it…then release it.

Shift your awareness to your left hand. Squeeze your fingers into a fist...then let it go. Turn your palm up and make a fist again, tensing your right forearm. Hold it for a few seconds, then release. Next, tense your upper left arm, pressing it in toward your rib cage. After a few seconds, let it go. Now tense your left shoulder and lift it up slightly, squeezing, holding...and releasing.

Turn your attention to your right hand. Make a fist...then relax your hand. Turn your palm up and squeeze your fist again, contracting the muscles in your right forearm. Feel the tension all the way to your elbow, then release. Next tense your upper right arm, as you did with your left. After a few seconds, release it. Now contract the muscles in your right shoulder and lift it up slightly, holding...then releasing.

Now focus on your neck and your throat. Drop your chin toward your collarbone, stretching the back of your neck and tensing the throat. Lift your chin releasing the tension. Open your mouth wide, stretching and tensing your jaw and lips. Then relax your jaw, leaving a gap between your teeth. Purse your lips and push them out like a kiss, then relax your lips. Curl your tongue to the back of your mouth, hold several seconds, then release.

Turn your attention to your eyes. Without moving your head, raise your gaze, then lower it toward your nose. Repeat several times. Then shift your gaze to the left, then the right. Back and forth several times.

Next, furrow your brow, tensing your forehead. Then open your eyes wide, stretching your forehead. Finally, relax your forehead, relax your face, relax your entire body. Stay focused and relaxed for as long as you wish.

Quick Scan

After you've become proficient at relaxing and letting go all the tension and stress, you might want to simplify your relaxation. Here's a shortened version allowing you to quickly slip into a relaxed state in preparation for meditation. For this method, you can either sit or lay on your back. You can sit on a cushion on the floor with your legs crossed, or you sit in a chair with your feet firmly planted on the floor. Take three deep breaths, each time slowly releasing the air.

Shift to gentle breathing and turn your head from side to side a couple of times. Imagine a wave of relaxation flowing down from the crown of your head over your face. Relax your jaw; relax your entire face. Bend your head side to side, stretching your neck. Then rotate your shoulders a couple of times.

Now, returning your focus to your breath, inhale deeply as you take four short sniffs. As you exhale, feel your entire body relaxing. Imagine a wave of relaxation flowing down your arms and out your hands....down your chest and back...down your hips, buttocks and legs, and out your feet. Repeat a couple of times, then shift to gentle breathing and enjoy the relaxing sensation.

Eventually, with practice, you will be able to quickly enter a relaxed state. You might be able to do so with a single deep breath, a slight twitch of your head or a roll of your shoulders, cueing your body to move automatically into relaxation.

The Relaxation Response

That's the title of a perennial bestselling book describing a relaxation technique. Written by Dr. Herbert Benson and published in 1975, the book's contention is that relaxation can counteract adverse effects of stress-related conditions, such as hypertension, anxiety, diabetes and even aging. The title of the book refers specifically to the response to the body's stress-related fight-or-flight mechanism.

Beginning in 1968, people involved in Transcendental Meditation (TM) repeatedly approached Benson at Harvard Medical School requesting that they be studied to show that relaxation and meditation could lower blood pressure. Initially,

Benson hesitated, but finally agreed to conduct the study. The publication of his book provided scientific support for relaxation and meditation.

While the technique he describes was drawn from Eastern meditation practices and is not original, Benson is credited with bringing the relaxation concept to the Western world and presenting it in a way that could be easily understood.

Interestingly, four decades after his original research, Benson was still active and in May of 2013 was listed as an author of a new study that supports his earlier work, and expands upon it. The research paper shows that relaxation can alter genes. Imagine that!

It describes the relaxation response as a physiological state of deep rest induced by practices such as meditation, yoga, deep breathing and prayer. The study found immediate changes in the expression of genes involved in immune function, energy metabolism and insulin secretion by those taking an eight-week course in the practice.

"People have been engaging in these practices for thousands of years, and our finding of this unity of function on a basic-science, genomic level gives greater credibility to what some have called 'new age medicine,'" wrote Benson, who is now director emeritus of the Benson-Henry Institute for Mind/Body Medicine.

Chapter 3

Mindfulness

"In this moment, there is plenty of time. In this moment, you are precisely as you should be. In this moment, there is infinite possibility."
—Victoria Moran

I work out in a gym a few times a week, something I've done for years as a complement to my yoga and meditation practice. I'm usually there mid-morning, and when I'm on the elliptical machine, the television in front of me is often tuned to the Jerry Springer Show. Thankfully, the sound is off and the frenetic behavior of the argumentative guests is accompanied by the music on my iPod.

I've heard other people on the nearby machines comment about the show, wondering why it's always on and isn't it just awful how the men and women get into fights on stage, and isn't Jerry Springer a sellout and a big jerk?

I don't think about the show that way. To me, it's an experiment in mindfulness. So what's that mean? How does Jerry Springer have anything to do with mindfulness and why is he even mentioned in a meditation book?

Before I answer, let's talk mindfulness. Usually it's not a good idea to define something by stating what it's not. But since mindfulness sounds suspiciously like filling your mind, I can't help but start out by saying: Forget that idea, because it is so wrong. Even if you fill your mind with knowledge and spiritual wisdom, that's not being mindful. On the other hand, mindfulness is not about emptying your mind, either. So what is it?

Scholars of Eastern philosophy have written extensively about mindfulness. After all, Buddha talked about it. In fact, mindfulness is part of the eightfold path of Buddhism. But anyone can practice mindfulness, a technique that has become a part of Western therapy to help us deal with anger, anxiety, stress, and all those feelings that take us away from happiness.

Being mindful is the ability to see things with new eyes, by experiencing the world without judgment. In order to do so, we have to overcome our inner dialogue, the chattering mind that constantly judges our experiences. While that judgmental process is important for survival, it also taints our view of reality.

When we pursue mindfulness, we remain in the present moment and pay attention to our thoughts and reactions. When we do so, we identify with the watcher. Remember our first exercise where I suggested that you just sit and let your mind do whatever it wants? Then I suggested trying to retrace your thoughts. That was cueing you to being mindful.

For me, The Jerry Springer Show is a test to see if I can remain mindful as I get an aerobic workout. In other words, I don't despise Springer or the nature of the show, nor do I enjoy it. It just is. Even though I have an opinion about the show, when I watch it in the gym I remain in the present moment, focused on my workout, and non-judgmental about what is showing on the television screen.

If I look up to the screen and see a woman slam another woman half her size to the floor as the audience cheers, I notice how I react. Am I disgusted, appalled, upset that the show is always turned on at this time, at this place? When I do that I'm paying attention to what I'm thinking. Being mindful. And I can quickly place the matter in perspective. It's a television show, it's entertainment. I don't let it bother me.

But what if two people in the gym suddenly started fighting, and one of them was my friend? Would I ignore what was going on? Of course not. The challenge then would be to do what I could to stop it without becoming enraged and joining the fray.

Likewise, how would I react if someone approached me and complained that I was on the machine too long and asked me sarcastically if I ever going to give other people a chance to use it? Again the challenge would be to remain aware of my reaction, whether I was being civil or reacting with anger. When you do that, you can quickly return to mindfulness, even if you temporary lost yourself in a defensive mode.

Thinking about Our Thoughts

Everyone knows about tongue-twisters, but what about *mind-twisters*? As humans, 'mind-twisting' is part of our nature. That's because we have the unique ability to think about our thoughts. Yes, thinking about thinking. And you probably thought that meditation was all about *not* thinking. Not exactly. You see, when we 'watch' our thoughts, so to speak, and place our mental state in the realm of the watcher, we start wondering, well, who's doing the thinking? Who's doing the watching? We begin to recognize a deeper part of ourselves, the watcher, the meditator—the true self. Through mindfulness this deeper part of ourselves begins to emerge, and we become more aware of the constantly changing nature of the world around us.

Before we move on to an exercise in mindfulness, I'll reiterate that little mystery of the mind. Here it is in a nutshell: Mindfulness is the awareness that is not thinking, but aware of thinking, as well as aware of how we experience the world. When we're mindful, we're paying attention on purpose and without judgment and with an open heart to whatever arises inside or outside of us. Of course, sometimes we trip up and let our emotions and attitude get the better of us. But we can always come back again into mindfulness.

Mindfulness leads to a greater awareness of whatever you are experiencing, whether you like it or not. Whatever the experience might be, you can find bliss in it by balancing the wisdom of the watcher with the desires of the chattering mind.

Take a few minutes to align yourself with the watcher in the following exercise.

Becoming the Watcher

Find a comfortable position, take several slow deep breaths, and feel your body relaxing as you exhale. Then slow your breath and with eyes closed take your time as you scan your body, relaxing it.

As you're doing the scan, remain aware of any thoughts that come to mind, literally 'watching' your thoughts. But don't fight your thoughts or get frustrated. Gently release your thoughts and return to your scan.

When you're done, stay focused on your breath, and again pay attention to your thoughts without getting carried away by them.

Notice what happens when you identify with the watcher, and stay in the present moment with an open heart. Pay attention to the chattering mind, without making any value judgments.

Typically, your thoughts tend to calm down as you pay attention to the internal dialogue. That's when you can find a space between two thoughts and move toward stillness and a state of meditation. Stay with it for at least ten minutes.

M-E-D-I-T-A-T-E

How did that work? Maybe you spent some time puzzling over the matter of watching your thoughts, and the idea that your true self is something other than your thoughts. In other words, you are not your thoughts.

Don't get annoyed or upset if you're not getting into a deep meditative state or are still uncertain what it is. Such emotions are hardly helpful. And don't be surprised if the watcher occasionally vanishes from your awareness as you get lost in your internal dialogue. As soon as that happens, you've merged with the active mind, lost your sense of mindfulness, and floated away down the river of thoughts. *Bye-bye.* But you can always come home and find your inner awareness again.

Speaking of coming home. When Steve Jobs returned from several months in India, he actually found it more difficult to re-integrate in American culture than overcoming the cultural shock he experienced when he arrived in India. He had discovered, to his surprise, that Western rational thought was not an innate human characteristic, but a learned one, and in the villages of India it was never emphasized. He's quoted in his biography, by Walter Isaacson:

"The people in the Indian countryside don't use their intellect like we do, they use their intuition instead, and their intuition is far more developed than in the rest of the world. Intuition is a very powerful thing, more powerful than intellect, in my opinion. That's had a big impact on my work."

That's quite a statement coming from one of the top technological innovators of our time—or any time! But there's more. Jobs recognized the difficulties we have in reaching a state of mindfulness.

"If you just sit and observe, you will see how restless your mind is. If you try to calm it, it only makes it worse, but over time it does calm, and when it does, there's room to hear more subtle things—that's when your intuition starts to blossom and you start to see things more clearly and be in the present more. Your mind just slows down, and you see a tremendous expanse in the moment. You see so much more than you could see before. It's a discipline; you have to practice it."

Mindful Walking

If you don't feel like sitting or lying down to meditate right now, you might practice mindfulness with a simple, slow, relaxed walk. Before you begin, take a few deep breaths, letting your upper body relax on the exhalation, then your lower body.

Set out on a specific path with a particular distance in mind, one that will take at least five minutes, but not more than fifteen or twenty. Let your arms hang loosely as you move forward with an easy gait. Bring your attention to the intricate movements of your body that we normally take for granted. Pay attention to how your heels touch down and you roll forward onto the ball of your foot as you lift up your other foot and swing your leg ahead.

Notice how all of your muscles, tendon and ligaments work together with your bones and your heart and lungs and brain to help you walk. Focus on all that you normally take for granted. Appreciate something in your surroundings, even if it's something small. Appreciate your ability to walk. Appreciate your life.

Pay attention to your breath and notice how it contributes to your ability to move forward. If you don't think your breath helps you walk, stop breathing for awhile and see how that works out. You won't walk very far before your body calls out for oxygen. Be conscious of every step and every inhalation and exhalation. Feel the air moving into and throughout your body, energizing you.

When your mind starts wandering, reel it in. Remain in the present moment on purpose, and stay focused on your walking. Keep an open heart and remain non-judgmental about walking.

Continue to appreciate. It doesn't matter what you are appreciating. The act of appreciation brings your attention to where you are right now.

Mindfulness vs. Meditation

In spite of the heading above, those two concepts are not really in competition with each other. Quite the opposite is true. They're actually in harmony, one complements the other. Since the terms are often used interchangeably, it's worth taking a closer look at the difference between the two.

Meditation varies from mindfulness in a number of important ways. It's a practice conducted at a set time and place, hopefully in a quiet setting. You might start your meditation by becoming mindful and paying attention to your thoughts and feelings. But gradually you want to go deeper toward inner experiences. You also might direct your meditations toward achieving particular goals. Such meditations usually involve visualization and inquiry, subjects we will get into in coming chapters.

Mindfulness, as I was saying, is about paying attention to the present moment—or present-moment awareness--doing so within an open heart, and without being judgmental. It's also the awareness that is not thinking, but aware of thinking, as well as aware of how we experience the world. It's the watcher that I've mentioned. It's cultivated by paying attention on purpose, deeply, and without judgment to whatever arises, either inside or outside of us.

The cool thing about mindfulness is that you can do it anywhere. You can practice mindfulness when you're alone or with others. Say you're at a party. Even in that environment, you can remain mindful. Watch what's going on. Notice what you're thinking, what you're saying, how you're acting, how you're feeling. Don't censor yourself, just pay attention. You might catch yourself being judgmental in your thoughts and words.

Imagine someone saying something offensive to you. Let's say that in the past you would get angry and insulted, and quickly attack. But if you can shift into mindfulness, aware of your thoughts and actions, you have an opportunity to respond in a new way, one that will defuse the situation rather than exacerbate it.

Of course, sometimes you might falter and let your emotions and judgmental attitude get the better of you. But you can always come back again into mindfulness. When you do, you'll find yourself much more in control of various situations that emerge during your day.

While mindfulness embraces open, expansive awareness of your surroundings as well as your feelings, meditation emphasizes narrow focused awareness and concentration. That's the key distinction.

Concentration

We concentrate when we read a book that really interests us, or watch a movie that captivates us, or work on a project that's really important and takes all of our attention. You can even become engrossed while shopping for shoes...or whatever.

But how do you concentrate while meditating? What happens? Concentration is different from focusing. Focusing is about narrowing your choices. Ie. Are you going to focus on your breath, a mantra or an affirmation? Concentration is about intensity... increasing the energy on whatever it is that you're focusing on.

Play with it

Try this experiment in concentration. Take a watch and stare intently at it for one minute. Count the number of times that your mind wanders off your concentration and into side thoughts about what you're doing and why you're doing it.

You can try something else right now to work on your concentration. Focus on the breath again, taking several long, slow deep inhalations and exhalations. Now concentrate on your breath. Nothing else matters. Stay with it. Several more deep breaths.... Now slow your breathing.

Turn inward by scanning your body. Concentrate on how your various body parts feel—start with your feet, your ankles, your lower legs, knees, thighs, hips and belly, your back, chest, shoulders, neck, your internal organs. Take your time.....feel your body relaxing. Stay focused and concentrate, intensifying your focus. Nothing else matters.

Now turn your concentration to your bodily functions. Maybe you become aware of the beat of your heart, the flow of blood from your heart, arteries, capillaries, and veins taking it back to your heart.

Go deeper. Concentrate. Listen again for the beat of your heart. Move your concentration into the flow of the blood through your body. Your heart, arteries, capillaries, veins moving the waste-rich blood back to the lungs and heart.

You might even go deeper into the self...beyond the physical into the invisible non-physical aspects of your beings, which is really your true self. Stay with it. Gentle breathing. Concentrating. Relaxing.

Finally, let it go. Bring yourself back to your normal awareness. How long were you gone? Now do you recognize the difference between meditation and mindfulness?

If you can't concentrate, you don't do well in life. Concentration allows you to remain entranced on whatever you're focused on. However, when you concentrate , you tend to tune out everything else. That's why some people, who excel greatly in one particular area, know very little about subjects outside of their expertise.

Mindfulness, on the other hand, provides an experience in expansive awareness, and the sense of being part of a universal web of awareness, interconnected with all that is. When you're mindful, you're in touch with the wonders of life that can nourish and heal, and expand your awareness.

Chapter 4

Breathe

"If you want to conquer the anxiety of life, live in the moment, live in the breath."

— Amit Ray

Oh, by the way, don't forget to breathe.

That's something I like to tell my meditation and yoga students. Of course, you don't need to remember. Your breath is on automatic drive. My point is to pay attention to your breath.

Sometimes it comes fast, as when you're involved in a series of yoga postures, such as the Sun Salutation, or any aerobic exercise. Or when you're excited or frightened. Other times your breath slows until it's barely perceptible, like when you're resting, but awake, as in *savasana* at the end of a yoga class.

In addition to automatic breathing, you can also control your breath, and in that sense breath-work is at the heart of meditation. It not only keeps you alive, but it provides a focus, an anchor, and serves as a connection to something greater. It's a means of staying in the present moment.

Prana

If you've taken classes in any traditional style of yoga, you've probably heard the instructor mention pranayama, a Sanskrit term for breathing exercises. At the base of the term is *prana*, which is sometimes confused with the air we breathe. It's much more than that. It's the life force — the sum total of all that keeps us alive. It's cosmic energy that connects everything in the universe. When we breathe, the vitality of the breath is prana.

In that sense, the process of breathing actually is much more than an essential body function. Nothing more than your breath connects you to the non-physical aspect of your being. As you relax and concentrate on the rhythm of your breathing, you trigger the vibrational frequency of a deeper part of yourself that exists outside of the everyday world. Mystics call it your soul, your spirit, your source. Your true self.

Some people are able to move into a state of deep meditation with little training. But most of us need to work with relaxation methods and breathing exercises.

Pranayama

Now that you've got a breath of fresh air about prana, let's explore a few breathing exercises. If you've taken yoga classes, you've probably been exposed to at least one of the following breathing methods. While the breath traditionally is considered at the heart of any yoga practice, instructors in some popular styles simply tell you to breathe, or be aware of your breath. If there is any emphasis on breathing methods in yoga classes, you're likely to have encountered the first of the following methods.

You can begin your meditation sessions with one of these breathing methods.

Ujjayi Breath

This technique is easily recognizable by the sound it produces, which varies from a soft hissing to a raspy breath. The sound is intentional, created by tensing the back of the throat on both the inhalation and exhalation.

Inhale through your nose, letting the air flow over the back of your throat, and listen to your breath. You might compare it to the sound of the sea or light snoring. Making a similar sound on the exhalation can be difficult at first. But if you exhale through your mouth, making a *ha* sound, you can create the same effect. Practice that method a couple of times, then simply bring your lips together on the exhalation and see if you can duplicate the sound, exhaling through your nose.

The sound itself is called *ajapa* mantra, which means the unspoken mantra. It serves to help slow your breath and focus your awareness on breathing. That makes it easier to prevent your mind from wandering. Practice for five minutes. Gradually, you can extend your breathwork to ten minutes.

M-E-D-I-T-A-T-E

The following breathing takes a bit more concentration, thus keeping you focused in the present moment.

4-Step Breathing

Begin by taking three deep inhalations and exhalations. Then for your next five breaths, inhale in four sniffs, gradually expanding the lungs. Empty your lungs with long, slow exhalations. After the fifth stepped breath, take three more deep breaths.

Next, take another long, slow inhalation, then exhale in four steps. Repeat four more times. Once again, take three deep inhalations and exhalations.

Now move into a stepped inhalation followed by a stepped exhalation. Four sniffs in, four sniffs out. Repeat four more times. Finally, take another three deep breaths as you finish the exercise. Notice how you've kept your attention on your breath, remaining in the present moment.

Diaphragmatic Breathing

This technique is especially good at the beginning of deep relaxation sessions while lying on your back.

As you inhale, round your belly. Exhale letting all the air out, allowing the belly to sink toward the spine. Deep belly breathing allows you to bring much more air into your lungs and oxygen into your blood stream and to all of your cells. As you inhale, the diaphragm contracts, moving downward, allowing more space for the lungs. At the same time, the rib cage expands out and up. As you exhale, the diaphragm relaxes and shifts upward, while the rib cage moves down and in.

Focus on your breath and the movement of your belly and entire torso. Feel your body relaxing on the exhalations. After three minutes, move into 3-part yogic breathing.

3-part Yogic Breathing

Begin the same way as diaphragmatic breathing, inhaling into the belly. Instead of exhaling, roll the 'bubble of air' up to the middle of your chest. Sniff in a little more air and roll it to the upper chest. Notice how your chest and shoulders tense. Then exhale slowly, relaxing.

Take another long, slow inhalation, repeating the same movement of the air. Pay attention to how the muscles in the abdomen and the chest come into play, and notice how this breathing method expands upon diaphragmatic breathing. Also, notice how it differs from step breathing, which doesn't involve the upward movement of the breath.

Spend three minutes with the method, then shift to gentle breath as you continue your meditation.

M-E-D-I-T-A-T-E

Alternate nostril breathing

Here's another method that occupies your mind, and your hand, and helps you remain in the present moment. But it offers much more than that.

Alternate nostril breathing, *nadi shodhana*, shifts the breath from one nostril to the other. In Yoga philosophy, the method is said to balance the left and right hemispheres of the brain, easing stress and anxiety. It also cleanses the nadis or channels of energy. In fact, the name comes from two Sanskrit words: *nadis*, meaning channels, and *shodhana*, which means cleansing or purifying. It's believed that when *prana* becomes unbalanced, due to mental and physical stress, the *nadis* are blocked, and that can lead to illness.

Begin in a seated position with your back straight, but not tensed. Bend your index and middle fingers of your right hand into your palm so that you can close off the right nostril with your thumb and the left nostril with the inside of your ring finger. If that feels awkward, then use your thumb and index fingers.

Close your right nostril and inhale through your left nostril. At the top of your inhalation close off both nostrils and hold your breath for a few seconds. Lift your thumb and exhale through your right nostril. Inhale through the right nostril and close both nostrils again. Hold a few seconds, then lift your other finger and exhale through your left nostril.

That's one cycle. Make your inhalations brisk and your exhalations long and slow. Repeat the cycle up to ten times. With practice, you can gradually increase the number of cycles. You can hold the inhalations longer before exhaling, and you can also close off both nostrils after exhaling and hold the exhalation a few seconds.

If you feel any dizziness during this practice, stop immediately and take several long, slow deep breaths. If you have high blood pressure, don't hold your breath at any time during the sequence.

When you're finished, lower your hand and breathe gently. Pay attention to your breath as you move into a deeper meditation.

M-E-D-I-T-A-T-E

Finally, here are a couple of breathing exercises that combine words with breath, and prepare you for the next chapter. The aim with this technique is to shift you into a relaxed state in a short time. It's a great method to use when you have very little time to meditate and your mind is buzzing.

Inhale Relaxation

Take five long, slow deep breaths. Then slow your breath, relaxing your body, focusing on your breath. You might see it as a white light flowing into your nostrils and lungs and out again. Remain mindful, but don't think of mindfulness as an exercise of effort or struggle, but instead think of it as a way of releasing and allowing, gently permitting yourself to be who-you-really-are.

When you become distracted by your thoughts, deepen your breath again, and add the following phrases.

Inhale relaxation, exhale tension;
Inhale health, exhale illness.
Inhale peace, exhale conflict.
Inhale abundance, exhale lack.
Inhale energy, exhale fatigue;
Inhale relaxation, exhale tension.
Inhale nothing, exhale let go.
Shift to gentle breathing. You're on your way into meditation.

Here's another breathing exercise, an ancient one, that combines sound and breath. The Hamsa Mantra, as it's known, actually mimics the sound of breathing. In a sense, you are chanting this mantra more than 21,600 times a day—the number of breaths you take on average.

The Hamsa Mantra

Hamsa is a Sanskrit term symbolized by a white swan, which flies between earth and heaven and joins them together. The swan represents freedom from bondage to the earth plane and the everyday world. This mantra supposedly predates Hinduism and Buddhism and it's speculated that Buddha used it in his meditations.

Softly whisper *ham* as you inhale, and *sa* as you exhale. Bring your lips together as you complete *ham*, which allows you to inhale through the nose. It can also be reversed, inhaling *sa*, exhaling *ham*. In this version, you're exhaling through the nose as your lips come together while you're saying *ham*.

Besides the mantra's relationship to the image of a swan, the two words can be interpreted. *Ham* means 'I' and *sa* means 'this'; literally, 'I am this,' or reversed, 'This I am.' Another interpretation is: 'I am that I am' or even, 'I am all that is.'

You might find one form energizing, and the other relaxing. You decide which it is. Close your eyes and notice the way your energy is altered while you inhale and exhale with *ham sa*, then reverse it with *sa ham*, and notice the subtle difference in the energy flow. In essence, the mantra balances masculine and feminine energy—stimulating in one mode, relaxing in the other.

Stay with the mantra for up to five minutes with each version. Remain in the present moment, mindful of your thoughts and gently returning to your breath. As you breathe, keep your attention on the internal sound of the mantra. Leave space between repetitions, moving into silence. Think of this mantra as a greeting to your inner self, your true self.

M-E-D-I-T-A-T-E

With practice, you'll find which version of the Hamsa Mantra that feels right for you at that moment.

Although the breath is always at the heart of meditation, words or phrases repeated over and over are another means of quieting the mind and staying focused. The next chapter on mantras and chants explores this method.

Chapter 5

Mantras and Chants

"Wave of the sea, dissolve in the sea. I am the bubble, make me the sea."
—Paramahansa Yogananda, *Cosmic Chants*

I think, but I am not my thoughts.
Think nothing.
All is well.
Let go.
OM…Love…One…God…Peace.

These are simple, generic mantras—words or phrases you can repeat to yourself during meditation. Mantras help you stay fully within the present moment. But they can also be a positive force that enhances your awareness. They literally take on a life of their own, one that guides and protects.

For example, early one morning I took a challenging vinyasa flow yoga class. Unlike most classes, this one was dominated by men. They were strong, flexible and all were more than two decades younger than me. They were also all at the front of the room, which meant these guys were not beginners, and were probably competent yogis.

There was a time when I regularly engaged in such classes. But over the years as the injuries—yes, some from yoga, others from varying activities—added up, my joints became more and more achy, especially in the morning. So here I was on my mat wondering if I was capable of making it through this decidedly macho yoga class.

Even before the class began, I started alternately repeating two related mantras to myself, one about healing, the other about success. I'll spell them out later in the chapter. The class started out slow and easy, but the pace and difficulty soon picked up. I pressed on, focusing on one mantra, then the other.

I noticed that after half an hour, one of the few women in the class was having trouble with some of the advanced strength-related poses. The next time I looked her way, her space was empty. I sympathized with her.

Finally, an hour and forty minutes after it began, the class ended. I'd overcome my aches and pains that included chronic knee and shoulder injuries. I actually felt quite good, especially since it was over! As I headed for the door, one of the women from the class turned to me. I recognized her as one of my former meditation students. "I see that you do more than meditate. Very impressive."

I smiled. "Actually, I *was* meditating."

Was it the power of the mantra that allowed me to get through the class without too much difficulty? You might think that a mantra itself is just words. Yes, that's true. However, when you apply those words, they gain power and produce results. The more you believe in that power, the more results you'll see.

Practice

Pick a simple mantra, a word or phrase from the list above or make up your own personal mantra, one that you can come back to again and again. Imbue it with power. Think of it as a magical spell, a guard helping you block out distracting thoughts and staying in the present moment. Put it to use.

Take several long, slow deep breaths, then shift to gentle breathing and begin saying your mantra to yourself. Say the mantra slowly, extending the word or words, such as *p-e-e-e-a-c-e*. Breathe in its power and notice how it absorbs all distracting thoughts. Feel it as if it were a dynamic, magnetic force.

Gradually, put more space between the repetitions, as you connect with a deeper part of yourself. When you realize you're thinking again, return to your mantra. Stay with it and keep increasing the space between repetitions.

When you become aware of your thoughts, let them drift by like fluffy white seeds from a cottonwood tree, floating away as you return to your mantra. Work with your mantra for five to ten minutes.

M-E-D-I-T-A-T-E

Seed Mantras

If I say, "squirrel," the word immediately translates to a small four-legged mammal with a bushy tail. Even my Golden Retriever knows that. In meditation, however, there are certain one-syllable words that don't represent anything. They're called seed mantras or *bija* in Sanskrit.

Thom Ashley-Farrand, author of *Healing Mantras: Using Sound Affirmations for Personal Power, Creativity, and Healing*, compares bijas to "the smell of a flower or the taste of an apple. Words don't define those experiences. The experiences define the words."

Bijas are easy to remember and recite, and they're also considered the most powerful mantras. Just as an acorn holds the capacity to grow into a giant oak tree and a mango seed can become a fruit-bearing tree, a bija contains condensed spiritual wisdom and creative power that can blossom over time.

Ancient Vedic texts are filled with stories of gods who used bijas to gain power. In a sense, a bija is the sonic equivalent to Harry Potter's wand or a shaman's totem animal. Any object of power can be a bija. Undoubtedly, the best known and one of the oldest of these seeds is *om*.

OM...AUM

It's the primordial sound of the universe, the vibratory power underlying all that exists. It's often called *pranama*, which means 'humming'. It's the sonic expression of the interconnection of all things. Om or AUM, as it is written in Sanskrit, connects and aligns us to universal energy. As a seed sound, om has no direct translation, but it's a sound that contains vast power.

The two spellings represent the fact that there are two ways of saying the mantra. You can pronounce it like room, extending the 'O' sound for a full exhalation, or you can pronounce the three-letter version, AUM, as *aahh...oohh...mmmm*.

'Ah' represents our waking state or everyday world, 'u' (pronounced "ooh") reflects the dreaming state, or inner awareness, and '*m*' is the dreamless state of deep sleep and the realm of ultimate unity.

As you chant this primordial sound, you move through the three states of consciousness to the mantra's 'after-sound,' the *anusvara*, or the silence that follows and symbolizes a transcendent state of consciousness, blissful, fearless, and enduring.

More Seed Mantras

Here's a list of seed mantras, their pronunciations, along with the god or goddess associated with each one, followed by the meaning of the mantra.

Select one of the seed mantras with the intent of making it part of your meditations. Pick one that feels right to you, that connects to energy you wish to bring into your life. Use it as a focus to help you let go of your busy mind. Repeat it throughout the day, anytime you have a few moments to quiet your mind.

If the one you picked doesn't feel right after the first day, try another one. Experiment and see if you can identify changes that come about after a couple of weeks. The more you repeat the mantra the more of its energy you pull into your life.

Shrim [shreem]: feminine; Lakshmi

The seed sound for abundance and prosperity. Any form of abundance applies, from financial wealth to spiritual riches. Other aspects of the shrim energy include inner peace, friendship and love of children and family life.

Gum [gum]: masculine, Ganesha

The masculine seed sound linked to Ganaesha, the remover of obstacles who opens the doors to success in your endeavors. Chew on that one for a while!

Dum [doom]: feminine

If fear is a concern, this mantra is the one to invoke. It's the seed sound for protection against anyone or anything that might cause you harm. You can make it part of your meditations and you can also chant it anytime that you feel fearful. The problem with this one for English speakers is the word looks like 'dumb' and sounds like 'doom.' But once you move past those cultural blocks, you can begin working with a powerful seed mantra.

Eim [I'm]: feminine; Saraswati

The seed sound for success in attracting spiritual knowledge. Eim encompasses artistic and scientific endeavors, music and education. It's also the mantra for improving memory and enhancing intelligence.

Krim [kreem]: feminine; Kali

Creation and destruction are two counter-forces that are combined within this powerful seed energy. It's about primordial feminine energy and can be called upon when you're intent on building power. Kali represents fierce energy and transformation. If you notice that you are feeling angry when working with this seed mantra, back off and try another one.

Haum [howm]: masculine, Shiva

Transcendental consciousness blossoms from this seed mantra. It's linked to Shiva, the personification of consciousness.

Klim [kleem]: neither masculine or feminine

The seed sound for attraction of what you desire. It's often combined with other mantras to achieve what you are seeking. For example, to achieve wealth, the mantra might go like this: *Om shrim klim*.

Kshraum [ksh-roum]: masculine, Narasimha-Vishnu

The seed sound for getting rid of on-going negative situations, and also for releasing pent up energies.

Hrim [hreem]: can be masculine or feminine

This seed sound is all about finding clarity and seeing through the illusions.

There are several other seed mantras associated with the chakras. See chapter 9.

Chants

Simply put, a chant is a mantra that you repeat aloud. More than a prayer, a chant can be compared to a packet of energy, knowledge and wisdom that's released within us. "When we chant sacred mantras, we are transformed and awakened to higher states of consciousness by the very nature and power of the sound," writes Robert Gass, author of *Chanting: Discovering Spirit in Sound*.

Most of the students who take my meditation classes are exposed to chanting for the first time and, not surprising, some say they find it monotonous. Yet, with practice, chanting moves beyond the tedium and can become a powerful vehicle for releasing blocked energy.

In yoga philosophy, chants—particularly those in Sanskrit— are said to enhance consciousness and stimulate a variety of energy frequencies. Every system of the body becomes infused with a vital life force, potent energy sometimes called chi energy, prana, or kundalini.

Chanting has been called *asanas* (yoga postures) of the tongue. Sanskrit chants, in particular, enhance our health and well-being by stimulating the pituitary gland, which is located just millimeters away from the roof of the palate. The pituitary gland governs our immunity system as well as our sexuality.

Chanting is also known to affect the vagus nerve, which passes through the neck and services the heart, lungs, intestines and intestinal tract and back muscles. The groundbreaking work of molecular biologist Candice Pert, author of *Molecules of Emotion*, reveals that emotional toxicity can remain lodged in the neuropeptides that line the walls of our intestines, because our breath is usually shallow. Since chanting naturally embodies cycles of deep respiration, much of this emotional toxicity can be released. Chanting, in other words, is a means of cleansing yourself of unwanted psychic residue, a process that has corresponding physiological effects.

Chanting is much simpler than singing and far more energizing than regular speech, notes Russill Paul, musician and author of *The Yoga of Sound: Tapping the Hidden Power of Music and Chant*. That's why spiritual traditions from around the world have successfully employed it in their religious lives and rituals of healing for thousands of years. "It is now ours to reclaim, reinvent, and reemploy this great gift to our species, aware that it has nothing to do with having a good voice or being musically competent," writes Paul.

As you go even deeper, you might start to feel that you are no longer chanting a mantra, but the mantra is chanting you!

Here are a few well-known chants. Pick one out and try saying it 108 times. That's a magical number in Eastern philosophies. Alternately, say it aloud for two minutes, whisper it for two minutes, then say it silently for two minutes. Eventually, expand to three minutes.

Sa Ta Na Ma

It's known as the Primal Sound Mantra, and is considered the most important meditation in Kundalini yoga. It signifies the eternal circle of life: Birth, life, death, rebirth. Each sound is said to have physical benefits. You can also use a finger motion with this chant:

For *Sa*, press the thumb and the index finger (or Jupiter finger) together with slight pressure; *Ta*, the thumb and the middle finger (Saturn); *Na*, the thumb and the ring finger (Sun); and *Ma*, the thumb and the small finger (Mercury).

For added meaning, the Jupiter finger brings in knowledge, expands your field of possibilities and releases you from limitations. The Saturn finger gives you patience, wisdom and purity. The Sun finger offers vitality and aliveness, while the Mercury finger enhances communication.

Om Namah Shivaya

It means 'I bow to Shiva,' and it's another well-known Sanskrit mantra.

Shiva is the supreme reality, the inner Self. It's your true identity, your soul's path. It's a powerful mantra, a chant about finding 'the watcher,' your true self. Hence, *Om Namah Shivaya* means "I bow to the Guru within."

The next two chants are slightly more complex. They are the ones I chanted over and over to myself during the challenging yoga class I mentioned earlier in the chapter.

Om Shri Dhanvantre Namaha
(OM SHREE DAN-VAN-TRAY NA-MA-HA)

This is the healing mantra, based on an appeal to the celestial healer, Dhanvantari, who gave the Nectar of Immortality to the gods. It can be used to enhance one's own healing skills, or for self-healing to promote healing on all levels: physical, mental or emotional.

Om Shri Ganeshaya Namaha
(OM SHREE GAN-EE-SHA-YA NA-MA-HA)

This mantra is for success, victory, prosperity, knowledge and illumination. It's hard to go wrong with that combination. It's definitely worth finding a few minutes of quiet time to chant this heady mantra.

It's also a chant for beginning meditation, starting new enterprises, or undertaking any new and good works. It's about breaking up obstructions.

Om Shrim Maha Lakshmiyei Swaha
(OM SHREEM MAH-HA LAKSH-MEE-YEI SHAH-HA)

This is the classic Sanskrit mantra for abundance, auspiciousness, and prosperity. *Shrim* is known as the seed sound for abundance. *Lakshmi* is the goddess who guides you, and *Swaha* is the divine feminine that represents receiving.

The Sanskrit words in this one might seem a bit intimating. But follow the pronunciation guide. Say it slowly at first. If you're still uncertain about how to say the word, you can Google the chant and listen to it on You Tube.

Om Mani Padme Hum

Of course, I can't forget this one. After all, it's how the book begins. If you read the introduction, you read all about it. Om Mani Padme Hum—the jewel within the lotus, which represents the mystery of life and transformation to a higher state of being.

I usually end my meditation classes with several minutes of

chanting, followed by three OMs, then finally an Irish Sun blessing, *Long Time Sun*. It goes like this:

May the long time sun shine upon you,
All love surround you.
And the pure light within you,
Guide your way home

One day I decided to download a copy of the song from iTunes. What prompted me to do so was a different version of the blessing that included a new second line about the 'cool moon.' I heard it recited at the end of a yoga class and afterwards asked the instructor about the line. The class had been taught on the day of the full moon, and she had led us through several variations of the moon salutation, instead of the usual sun salutation.

So I thought that she might've just added the line about the moon for the purpose of the class. She laughed at that idea and assured me that the line was part of the Irish Sun Blessing, and that no, she had not made it up.

So the next day, which happened to be St. Patrick's Day, I looked it up on iTunes, and listened to seven or eight variations. But not one of them included a line about the moon. After all, it's a sun blessing. I particularly liked the rendition sung by a Kundalini yogini Snatam Kaur, who has recorded several albums of sacred music.

However, no matter how many times I tried, I couldn't download the song. The tune was frozen, wouldn't play, and wouldn't download. I shrugged it off, but the next day I went back and found the same situation. The song would not download for me. So I started puzzling over the esoteric meaning of it all.

Then it came to me. As I said, the previous day had been St. Patty's Day. Not only had I tried to download the Irish blessing without any conscious recognition of the connection, but I had spent the entire day without wearing anything green. An inadvertent snub of the Irish, I suppose, and maybe the freeze had been my payback!

Meditation Joke #2

Here's another joke, one with a pointed message. It deals with the issue of pronunciation of Sanskrit words. Yes, that's a strange topic for a joke, but here goes.

A scholar studied Sanskrit and meditation practices for years. He became an expert. He practiced meditation daily. He chanted for hours. He read every book available on the subject and memorized passages from ancient texts. He was highly regarded, and thought he knew almost everything there was to know about the subject.

Then one day he heard about a hermit who lived in a cave on an island. He was supposedly a highly advanced meditator, knowledgeable and wise. So the scholar journeyed to the lake and hired a boatman to ferry him to the island for a day trip. When he arrived, he hiked along a trail through the jungle until he found the hermit's cave.

The hermit was meditating in the candlelit cave when the scholar interrupted him. To his relief, the hermit seemed pleased to have a visitor and invited the scholar to join him in chanting a sacred mantra. The scholar knew this mantra very well and was happy to chant with the hermit.

However, after less than a minute of chanting, the scholar stopped and waved his hands. Horrified, he explained to the hermit that he had wasted all of his years on the island. He was mispronouncing the Sanskrit so his chants were meaningless and without power.

The hermit listened closely to the proper way to pronounce the words and thanked the scholar for correcting him. The scholar left, disappointed, and as the boatman rowed away from the island, the scholar told him how sorry he felt for the poor hermit. Suddenly, the boatman pointed and gasped.

The hermit was running across the surface of the water toward the boat. As he reached the craft, he again thanked the scholar and asked if he would repeat the proper pronunciation again. The astonished scholar was dumbfounded. "If you can do *that*, then you are doing fine."

"Oh, but I want to improve myself. Please say the chant again." The baffled scholar did so, and the hermit raced back to the island, reciting the chant, his feet barely dipping into the water.

The meaning behind the joke, of course, is that proper pronunciation of Sanskrit mantras is not essential. In fact, no matter how hard you try, you probably won't get it right. Except for a mere 14,000 people who consider Sanskrit their native tongue, it's a classical language—a dead language, like ancient Greek—that mainly exists in the realm of devoted scholars and yogis.

Chapter 6

Affirmations

An affirmation opens the door. It's a beginning point on the path to change.
—Louise L. Hay

A sticker on the back of my car reads: *If anything good can happen, it will.*

To me, that seems like a simple, clear-cut message: an affirmation. Yet, on several occasions people in parking lots have pointed to it and asked what it means, or just said they didn't get it. To explain, I ask if they'd heard Murphy's Law: *If something can go wrong, it will.* Yes, of course, they respond. My bumper sticker is the inverse of Murphy's Law as well as its popular corollary slogan, *Sh*t Happens*.

Certainly we can sympathize with the stories of those who have experienced the full force of Murphy's Law. But there's no reason to wear the slogan as an honor and wait for the next chance to confirm its truth. Try the opposite.

Like mantras, affirmations are words of power that can help you focus and remain mindful. While the two terms are sometimes used interchangeably, mantras tend to focus on spiritual awareness and enhancement. Affirmations, on the other hand, are often more worldly, and related to positive thinking and self-improvement.

Affirmations are intentions, things or states of being that you are intent on achieving. They are something you do to attract positive energy to accomplish goals. You repeat them to yourself, focusing on your intention and doing so with confidence and joy. You can say affirmations to yourself as part of meditation or anytime during your day. You can repeat them as you walk across parking lot, while you're grocery shopping, even while your eating a meal. You embed them in your mind.

The very process of repeating an affirmation can help you feel less stressed and anxious, more confident and creative. They help you deal with negative feelings, such as frustration, guilt, anger, shame, fear or disappointment. More than feel-good statements, they serve as a means of shifting your awareness, and changing all that you want to change.

The more exhilarated you feel, the more likely your affirmation will come to pass. For example, if you're nervous about an upcoming talk to a group of strangers, you might say: "I enjoy telling my story to new people, and I do so with confidence and enthusiasm." You might write that phrase on your computer fifty times, text it to a friend, print it out and tape it to your refrigerator, shout it while you're in the shower or stuck in traffic. Feel it, believe it, and know it works.

What is it you want?

Affirmations aren't just wishful thinking; they are acts of wish-fulfillment.

Years ago, when my wife Trish and I quit our jobs and set out on a freelance writing career, many of our friends, former colleagues and family thought we were chasing an impossible dream. We knew that some people succeeded as writers and, working together, we could do it, too. But we needed to act in ways that would impress our goals and desires on our minds. Hard work and positive thinking was part of it. So we repeated affirmations and practiced visualizations, the subject of the next chapter. We were intent on becoming successful writers and we affirmed our specific goals over and over.

We focused on that new reality as if it had already happened, and of course we kept writing. Did it work? We've published more than 100 books, both novels and non-fiction. Our books have been published in more than a dozen languages, we've won writing awards, and have made a living as writers for more than 30 years. We're still at it, still affirming.

Like us, you probably want something that's missing in your life. Pinpoint it. If it's just a general idea, try to be more specific. What is it you want now? Right this instant?

Formulate Your Affirmation

Always use the present tense. In other words, don't say: *Wonderful things are soon coming for me*. Focus on now, not the future, not on any time-frame. That provides an immediacy. Pretend your affirmation is already here. *Wonderful things are happening in my life.*

What kind of wonderful things? Is it about your career, your love life, finances? Then get even more specific. Instead of saying, *Wonderful things are happening in my career*, you might add: *I get a promotion and a raise.*

Stay positive. Focus on what you want, not what you don't want. Don't say: *I'm not going to stay in this lousy job.* Instead, you might say: *I now have new opportunities to advance my career.*

Feel it and accept it

Enjoy your new reality, even if you can't see it yet.

Focus on what you want rather than what you lack. Emphasize the positive and accept the idea that you already have achieved your goal. You made it! You did it! Rejoice!

Dr. Joe Dispenza, author of *You are the Placebo: Making Your Mind Matter*, puts it this way: "When you're truly focused on an intention for some future outcome, if you can make inner thought more real than the outer environment during the process, the brain won't know the difference between the two. Then your body, as the unconscious mind, will begin to experience the new future event in the present moment. You'll signal new genes, in new ways, to prepare for this imagined future event."

Intention, Attention, No Tension

Here's a mantra to help you solidify your affirmation once it is firmly fixed your mind. Take your usual meditation position, preferably seated in a quiet space where you won't be bothered. Take a few deep breaths, then relax your body from head to foot.

When you feel at ease and are moving into a meditative state, focus on your affirmation. Say it to yourself with conviction. Repeat it for about a minute. Notice your thoughts, but don't get caught up in them. Remain mindful.

After a couple of minutes, with your affirmation in mind, say to yourself: *Intention, attention, no tension.* You're intending your affirmation, then giving it attention, finally releasing it. Yes, it's important to let it go, send it on its way, and trust that the Universe will take care of it.

Spend at least five minutes repeating the mantra. Know that your affirmation has been heard and will be answered.

Take it with you

Affirmations are like mindfulness in that you can take them with you. You can be mindful at any time and any place. Likewise, affirmations travel well. Write your affirmation by hand and carry it around in your pocket. Take it out into your day and repeat it often, imprinting it on your mind.

Give thanks over and over. Be appreciative for what you have.

Putting it to Memory

Whenever you have self-doubts and something disturbing happens, you might invoke a memorized affirmation. Here are some possibilities.

- I am here in this present moment to bring joy into my life.
- Every day in every way I'm getting better and better.
- I am relaxed and focused. I am here to seek higher experiences. I am guided and protected.
- I am here in the hopes of becoming more centered and aware, more grateful and happy, and willing to bring more light and happiness to others.
- I flow as easily as the wind blows through the sky above. All the blessings I need flow effortlessly into my life.
- I love and approve of myself.
- I'm filled with confidence and hope, and have no time for self-pity and surrender.
- I am loved and appreciated.
- I am making the right choices every time.

- I'm drawing on my strength and inner light.
- I am unique and well qualified, and have much to offer the world.
- Wonderful thing are unfolding for me.

You can also combine your affirmations with visualization. We'll explore that subject in the next chapter.

Chapter 7

Visualization

"I would visualize things coming to me. It would just make me feel better. Visualization works if you work hard. That's the thing. You can't just visualize and go eat a sandwich."

—Jim Carey

What you see is what you get.

No doubt you've heard that saying. Typically, it's said as a way to lower expectations. In other words, don't expect too much. But alter the words slightly to read: *What you get is what you see*, and now the phrase takes on new meaning. It's about visualization or mental imagery...making things happen, seeing the impossible, the improbable, and with new eyes watching it manifest.

But what is this other way of seeing? How do you do it? Most likely you already do it without thinking about it. When you dream, do you see images? Do you hear voices? When you read a novel, do you imagine what the characters look like? These are a couple of ways that we visualize. In meditation, visualization is one way of focusing the mind and it's often done with a particular intention in mind, such as achieving a goal, healing yourself, deep relaxation, making contact with spirit guides, or exploring inner realms.

Of course, the best way to understand visualization is to practice this method of focusing. Let's start with a simple test to get a sense of how well you already visualize. You can try it by reading each item, then closing your eyes and visualizing. Alternately, you might record the following list, leaving fifteen or twenty second of silence between each one. Or, if convenient, have someone read the phrases to you.

The Mind's Eye

Move into your place of meditation and take a few deep breaths as you consciously relax your body. Then slow your breath and take one phrase at a time. Close your eyes and visualize:

… a yellow triangle

…a blue circle

… a bowl of red strawberries.

…a brilliant sunset with pink and orange clouds

…a watermelon sliced open lengthwise, notice the color and texture

…a line of pelicans gliding along the coast at dusk

….a snow-capped mountain in the distance

….a full moon over the ocean…smell the air

…a large black stallion with a shiny coat…see it rear up.

….finally, a lemon cut in half, see it, smell it, taste it

Were you able to sense the images? How clear were they? Some people are adept with images and can see them with their mind's eye as if they were looking at a picture, or watching a movie. They can easily see a stallion rear up, kicking it's legs and hear it whinnying. They can see it with their eyes open or closed. Others might only get a fleeting glimpse of the object in question.

If you're having difficulty seeing an image, it could be that you're not familiar with the target object. For example, if you've never seen a line of pelicans gliding along the coast at dusk, it could be challenging to visualize it. Test yourself with a familiar image. Think of someone you know well, a partner, a child or a parent, a good friend. Breathe, relax, close your eyes, and think of the person. Can you see his or her face? Do you at least get a flash of features?

Another reason you might have difficulty seeing an image is because you might not be relaxed enough. Think about when you're falling asleep and images appear. Some people in that hypnogogic state, between sleep and wakefulness, can consciously describe what they are seeing. In that borderland state, they can function in both worlds to some degree.

If you jot down the images that you're seeing, you'll have an easier time remembering them as such images are often fleeting. When you do so, you're recalling what it's like to see images with the mind's eye. However, those images are manifested from the unconscious mind. In visualization, you are consciously creating the images.

Manipulating Images

Can you play with images in your mind, shifting them into new shapes? Take a moment to picture the full moon. Now telescope the image, zoom in so you can see crater-pocked surface of the glowing sphere. Easy, right?

Try this one: Imagine a lime-green VW Beetle, then make it bright yellow with a convertible top and shiny wheels. Maybe you can do this, but you wonder, *what's the point?*

We'll get to that. Here's a hint. Take out a dollar bill and examine the front side. Put it aside, close your eyes and see the bill in your mind. Imagine that it's crispy and new. Now, change the image on the bill from Washington to Ben Franklin and notice that the number in the corners is 100 rather than 1. You've just transformed a dollar into a hundred dollars. At least in your mind...and that's where it all starts.

Visualization in Action

The sports arena is probably where visualization has had its most noticeable impact. Many star players in various sports endorse the practice. Some proponents have even said that success in athletics is ninety percent mental and ten percent skill.

Russian scientists, in a widely quoted study, compared four groups of Olympic athletes. In the first group, the athletes spent 100 percent of their training time in physical activity. The second group spent 75 percent of their time in physical training and 25 percent in mental imaging. The third group divided their time equally between physical and mental training, while the fourth group spent 75 percent of their time in mental training and 25 percent in physical training.

When tested, the fourth group, which spent the majority of its time training in mental imagery, performed the best.

Athletes practice visualization to improve performance skills and problem-solving, gain confidence and bolster their positive thinking. They also use visualization to control anxiety, particularly just prior to performing. They might mentally recreate the feeling of winning or achieving their top level of performance. They might see themselves excelling beyond all expectations, and imagine hearing the crowd cheering them on. They might visualize how they would look and feel when they achieve their goal.

Alternate Senses

Some people are not so visually oriented and do better at feeling or hearing or smelling than seeing. Let's work with some other senses now.

Close your eyes, and take a couple more deep breaths. Now imagine it's pleasantly cool outside with temperatures in the mid-50s. It's night and you're standing by a campfire or a fire pit. Take a look at it. Do you see the flames? Red, orange, yellow. Watch the flames flicker against the night.

Move a little closer to the fire. Can you feel the heat? One of the logs pops, sending up a shower of sparks, another log crackles. Can you hear the pop and the crackle? Now the wind shifts and smoke blows your way. Can you smell the sooty smoke and sense how it feels in your eyes? Back away and it's not so hot and you feel the cool night air. You can still see the fire, but it starts to fade away and then disappears.

Open your eyes. How did that work? Were you able to pick up multiple senses? Did one sense work better than another?

That exercise should help with our next visualization, which uses imagery for relaxation.

Breathing in the Images

While you're seated or lying down, focus on your breath. Gradually deepen your breathing, inhale through your nose and tense the back of your throat. Listen to your breath, which should sound like light snoring or the sound of the sea. Exhale through your nose and see if you can make a similar sound.

That's called *ujia* breathing. As you breathe, visualize ocean waves breaking onto the beach, then washing out. Imagine a wave breaking on shore as you inhale, washing out as you exhale. Stay with that image and with that rhythm for several breaths.

Now slow your breath as you expand the visualization. See yourself lying on the beach near the shore. It's a beautiful day, just the right temperature. Let yourself relax. The sand forms a mold of your body. A gentle wave breaks in and washes over your feet and ankles, then retreats. A few easy breaths later, another wave comes in and flows over your feet and lower legs, then slips away.

Follow the flow and ebb as the water gradually washes over your belly, then slides out. Let yourself relax, and enjoy the feel of the warm healing waters washing over you. Notice that the blue sky is immense from horizon to horizon. The sky represents your mind—beautiful, broad and clear. Now imagine the sun as a source of great healing and nourishment.

Relax and stay with the image for a few minutes.

M-E-D-I-T-A-T-E

Here's another visualization exercise, one which allows you to release the burdens you are carrying. It's one that you might want to record and play back during meditation. Alternately, someone might read it to you as you mediate or you might read it to someone else who is meditating with you.

Balloon Meditation

After you are settled in and relaxed, imagine you're standing in a wide open field on a beautiful day. You can see cows in the distance eating grass. You hear the buzz of insects and the chatter of birds. You feel the warmth of the sun. Then you notice a hot air balloon landing in the field. Look closely at it as you walk over to it. What color is it? Are the colors solid or striped? How large is it?

As you move closer, you notice that the balloon's basket is empty, and that this is an unusual balloon. You realize that you have a chance to unload all of your problems, worries, concerns, and fears into the basket. You can let go of all the weight on your shoulders from things that happened in the past, old injuries, both physical and mental ones. If someone offended you, put it in the basket. If you offended someone else, place any left over sense of guilt into the basket.

Now watch the balloon lift off, taking away all that load you were carrying. Feel a sense of lightness, a new freedom. You've been unburdened, released. Now relax.

But make sure that you really let it go. There might be a line attached from the balloon to your solar plexus. It represents doubt… doubt that you can let it all go. All it takes is one tug on that line and it's released and now you truly let go of all that stuff. Sit quietly a few moments, watching the hot air balloon drifting farther and farther away.

For the next five to ten minutes, remain relaxed, your mind calm. Let any distracting thoughts drift away with the balloon.

M-E-D-I-T-A-T-E

The X-Factor

The next exercise provides an important clue to making your visualizations manifest in the everyday world. You could call it the X-factor or the magical ingredient. You have to accept whatever it is you're visualizing before you can experience it. If it's something that you want to change in your life, then you must feel that it has already happened. If it's something you desire, then believe that you already have it. One of the best ways for accepting something you seek is by offering profuse thanks for it. The more you are thankful for it, the more you appreciate it, the more likely it is that it will become part of your life.

Simply put: See it, believe it.

As I was considering how to close this chapter, the 'blog angel' came to my aid when I clicked onto a friend's blog. I was amazed to see that Mike Perry of Cornwall, England had just written a post on visualization in which he talked about putting the 'library angel' to work by randomly selecting a book off a shelf of his library, opening it and reading from the page.

He picked *Practical Application Of Science Of Mind* and this is what he read: "… for unless we accept it we are rejecting it; and if we are rejecting it we are not believing that we have it; and while we believe that we do not have it the Law cannot make a gift. Hence, we are told to believe that we already possess the object of our desire, and so should make known our request with thanksgiving."

In other words, give thanks for all that you desire, as if it were part of all that you possess, all that you are. It seems that all things are possible: happiness, love, money, peace of mind as long as we believe that we already have happiness, love, money, peace of mind.

With *affirmations*, we create a message and send it out to the Universe. With *visualization*, we create images to enhance our affirmations. With *inquiry*, the subject of the next chapter, we send out questions to the Universe and watch for answers. It's a kind of conscious dreaming.

Chapter 8

Inquiry

"As human beings we are all capable of inquiry, of discovery, and this whole process is meditation. Meditation is inquiry into the very being of the meditator."

—J. Krishnamurti

In the search for extra-terrestrial life, radio signals were sent out in into our galaxy with a message for other civilizations to contact us. That was forty years ago and we've been waiting and watching ever since for a reply to the Arecibo message, as it is known. Inquiry is something like that, except you're sending your message to *inner space*, not outer space, and you don't need all that high-tech equipment. You ask a question and watch for an answer through images or voices or other sensations. Essentially, inquiry is a kind of conscious dreaming, and allows us to look deeper within. Hopefully, you won't have to wait as long as the astronomers for a response.

When you pose a question during meditation, you might wonder who are you asking. That depends. Such an experience can lead to encounters with a deeper part of yourself, mythical or religious figures, spirit guides, or Source energy. It all depends on your perspective and your intention.

Let's move right into it with a meditation involving inquiry, deep relaxation and visualization.

Enhanced Awareness

Start your meditation by selecting a question that you want answered. It might be one of the big questions, such as: *What is my purpose in life*? Or, *What will I be doing in five years*? Make your question significant and personal. Look for the emotional context.

What is your core issue? Is it about fear, self-worth, insecurity, an emotional block? For example, if you want to change your career, what is keeping you from making the move? Is it a fear that you won't succeed? An uncertainty about what you really want to do? Your question might be: *What's keeping me from changing my career?*

As you search for the core issue, you might touch upon something that causes you to react by thinking: *No, not that, anything but that.* Perhaps you asked, *What is it about me that people dislike?* Or, *Why do I keep getting fired?* Or, *Why am I ignored?* If that happened, you've probably found your core issue. Here's an opportunity to confront it and find a resolution. Take your time and phrase your question carefully. Think about it awhile.

When you've decided on your question, you can begin again by taking several deep breaths, slowly inhaling and exhaling through your nose. Next, slow your breath and feel a sense of relaxation flow down your body from the crown of your head, along your torso and your limbs to your hands and feet. Relax, relax, relax.

Take a few minutes to relax deeper, paying attention to your breath or a word or phrase.

When you're fully relaxed, re-state your question to yourself. You're going to be taking a journey to a special power chamber where you will experience enhanced sight, feelings and hearing.

Imagine that it's dusk now and you see a tall circular building, like a tower, perched upon the side of a mountain or hilltop. You see steps leading up to the building. You approach and slowly climb the stone stairs. You feel the coolness of the air and notice your exertion, the beat of your heart. You hear the call of a solitary bird from high above as if announcing your arrival.

You reach the base of the building and see an elevator in front of you. As you approach, you hear humming and soft hissing as the doors slide apart. You step inside. The doors close and you feel yourself rising. You hear a soft voice slowly counting. 1…2…3…4…5….6…7…8…9…10. The elevator stops and you step into a circular chamber. The walls are dark, the lighting low. Move over to a reclining chair in the center of the chamber and settle into and relax.

Suddenly, the wall glows a soft red. Now the walls shift to orange, then the tone changes to yellow...green...blue...purple...violet. Now you're ready to receive a response to your question. Say your question to yourself again and let the answer unfold at its own pace. It might reveal itself as a movie with you or someone else playing the main role. It could even occur at another time and in a distant place.

Don't worry if it seems like your imagination. Go with it, see where it takes you. Later, you can review the movie and interpret the message. Maybe your answer will be more direct. Someone might appear and offer advice. Note how this person looks and pay attention to what is said. Or, you might just hear a voice. Listen closely and know that you will remember everything that you were told. Alternately, if your inner sight and hearing don't play a role, you could receive feelings and impulses that impart an important message. You'll know what these feelings mean, and how to interpret them.

Inhale deeply a couple more times. Take time now to watch, listen or feel your answer.

M-E-D-I-T-A-T-E

After ten or fifteen minutes, slowly come back to your normal awareness. The power chamber gradually fades away, but you'll remember everything that happened there. Count slowly from 1 to 5 and with each number you'll feel happier and more awake. 1...2...3...4...5. You're back. Did you get your answer?

Looking for 'I'

An essential part of being humans involves an awareness of 'I.' Without it, we lose our identity, what makes us individuals. It also creates a sense of separateness that Buddhists call an illusion. And that's true if we consider the physical world as a projection of non-physical or spirit realms, where everything is connected. That underlying reality is the domain of 'Indra's Net,' a metaphor of Hindu origin for the sense of interconnectedness of all things where one tug on the net ripples throughout the Universe.

During deep meditation, we can peer through the veil from our everyday world where so much seems separate and unrelated to the deeper reality that exists outside of cause and effect, outside of the sense of separateness. We can experience an expansion of self, but not an annihilation of the personal self. We experience both individuality and unity, not as opposites, but part of the whole self.

Here's another meditation, using inquiry and looking for answers about the self.

Who am I?

Settle down into a relaxed state following whatever procedures you've established. Maybe you need to undertake a full body scan, taking your time as you relax each part of your body. Alternately, maybe you can quickly scan your body as you relax. But don't rush it, especially if your busy mind is still buzzing from the day's activities or you're feeling stressed.

When you're ready to proceed, focus on this simple, yet complex question: *Who am I?*

Say it over and over to yourself. Use it as your mantra as well as your question, the focus of your meditation. Stay with it. Return to it when your mind wanders. Remain open to receive answers that might come as a vision, a voice, or some other sensory input.

Watch for symbols to appear that you can interpret. Two of my students, Lisa and Richard, told me after class about the images they had seen. Lisa glimpsed her wedding ring being pulled from her finger. That was an obvious symbol of the end of her marriage, which had been in its death throes for months. She realized that the person she was becoming was someone in transition, undergoing major changes in her life.

Richard saw himself on a treadmill that was moving faster and faster, and he knew exactly what that meant. His career was on a fast track. He had a high-pressure job and no matter how hard he worked there was always more to do. The meditation made him realize how little time he had for himself, and prompted him to think about an alternative career that would be more rewarding.

Contemplation

If your daily life is busy, you too might feel like you're running on a treadmill. You can speed up or slow down, but it never seems to stop. However, you can step off the treadmill and reflect on where you're going, what you're doing, and what you want. It's a form of meditation called contemplation and it can be an empowering experience, allowing you to take more control over your life. It involves deep reflection on your life while in a relaxed meditative state. You can listen to yourself and make contact with your intuition, ask questions and watch for answers.

You might start out by writing in a journal. The process of writing enables you to turn inward and reflect. As you write, you can shift from thinking to contemplation.

Begin your journaling by taking a few slow deep breaths, relaxing as you exhale. You might start with a question or intention, some issue on your mind, a worry or concern, possibly something you're anxious about. *Why do I keep doing this? How can I change?* Maybe it's about a relationship, a health matter, finances or a job or career issue. It could be a desire or wish, maybe a goal you have in mind.

But don't worry about it, because that doesn't help. Just formulate a question or statement—your intention—something you want to know. Write whatever comes to mind. Let one thought flow into another and see where they go.

When you're done writing, contemplate the matter. Notice how you feel about it. Are you annoyed, excited, wary, angry, sad? Pay attention to your feelings in the same way that you notice your thoughts. It's as if you're outside your thoughts and feelings, watching them.

You've set your intention or question. You've given it attention. Now let it go. Release it. Let it float away.

Repeat your question or intention again. Give it some attention. Then release it. Watch for answers to appear. They might come to you as a vision, a whisper, a sensation. Or perhaps the answer will come in another way. For example, a book falls to the floor and you pick it up and randomly select a page and read a line or paragraph, and what you read is meaningful, an answer to your question, or a confirmation of your intention.

Or, maybe no answer appears. You get up and make something to eat or take a shower, or a nap. And suddenly, there's the answer. It comes to you when you least expect it.

Here's another joke, one that deals with inquiry. In this case, the question was: *What was that?*

Meditation Joke #3

Three master yogis were meditating in a cave high in the mountains. They'd been there several years when one day, they hear a sound of clattering rocks at the entrance to their cave. They continue their silent meditation nonplused.

Six months later, one of the monks clears his throat and says: "That was a donkey."

A year passes in silence until the second monk retorts: "No it wasn't. It was a goat."

Two more years go by, and finally the third monk speaks. "If you two don't shut up, I'm leaving."

CHAPTER 9

Chakras

"And, in the end, the chakra system in our bodies is how we find our way back to the most ancient mystery of all — God, the Oneness, the Omniscient."
—Rosalyn L. Bruyere, *Wheels of Light*

You'll never read about them in *Gray's Anatomy*, the best known book on human physiology. But chakras are part of an ancient tradition that were described in the *Vedas*, the oldest written documents of India, dating back to 1,500 B.C. They were recorded from oral tradition by upper caste Brahmins, who may have been descended from the Aryan stock that migrated into India from the north.

In spite of its ancient roots, chakras were virtually unknown in the Western world until an Englishman, Arthur Avalon, described them in *The Serpent Power,* published in 1919. He referred to a tenth century text, the *Padaka-Pancaka,* that included descriptions of the energy centers and related practices. Another tenth century text, called the *Gorakshashatakam,* gives instructions for meditating on the chakras.

Meditation and chakras are as intertwined as shoes and socks. You don't always need to wear socks — especially if you're walking in sandals—and of course you don't always need to focus on chakras when you meditate. However, meditation is a great means of expanding your awareness of these invisible energy centers that exist in a 'subtle body,' that surrounds your physical body. Theories about the subtle body and chakras date back to the distant past in Eastern philosophy.

You might intellectually understand the concept of chakras— their locations in relationship to the body, their colors and Sanskrit names—but through meditation you can experience the nature of these energetic fields.

However, before we get into a chakra meditation, let's cover the basics. Chakras consist of seven power points of life force depicted in ancient Hindu and yoga texts as spinning vortexes of energy. In fact, Chakra is a Sanskrit word meaning 'wheel' or spinning wheel.

Chakras span the body from the base of the spine to the crown of the head, and correspond to the seven main nerve ganglia that emanate from the spinal column. Each chakra is associated with a particular color and sound.

A chakra meditation is about tuning the chakras. It's like getting the wheels on your car aligned. It brings you more into balance, bring more energy and balance into your life, a meditation of self-healing.

Let's take a tour of the seven chakras, with a meditation of 2-5 minutes for each. Takes several deep breaths, and feel your body relaxing with each exhalation. Then shift to gentle breathing.

FIRST CHAKRA
Root chakra, Muladhara, your foundation

Your first chakra is located at the very base of your spine, and is your grounding chakra, connecting you to the earth energy and is associated with the adrenal glands. Basic survival is handled in the first chakra, and it can give you sudden bursts of strength and energy when you need it. It's also about stillness. When the root chakra is blocked an individual may feel fearful, anxious, insecure and frustrated.

The root chakra is associated with the color red. Imagine a bright red apple hanging on a tree. Pay attention to the color. Now imagine the root of the apple tree spread deep underground, anchoring the tree into the earth. Imagine that you have invisible roots just like that tree. These roots enable you to draw into your body the positive frequency of the mother earth.

You are now beginning to feel the awareness of a reaction from the planet deep below the surface coursing into your being. As your roots entwine with the Earth energy, use your senses to experience the awareness of unconditional love and healing. Focus on the color red and you might quietly hum the musical note C, the Do of the Do-Re-Mi song.

M-E-D-I-T-A-T-E

SECOND CHAKRA
Sacral chakra, swadhisthana, creativity, sexuality

Your second chakra is situated just below your naval and is associated with the sex organs. This chakra is identified with your center of emotions, vitality, creativity, fertility, reproduction and sexual energy. When this chakra is out of balance, it's reflected in emotional problems, especially fears nervousness or sexual guilt. You might be obsessed with security issues and resist change.

The sacral chakra is associated with the color orange, a high-energy color. Its juices are extremely intoxicating and sweet tasting. Tune your second chakra by visualizing a ripe orange filling the screen in front of your vision. You could hum the musical note D or Re.

M-E-D-I-T-A-T-E

THIRD CHAKRA
Solar plexus chakra, Manipura, self-empowerment

Your third chakra is located at your solar plexus, between your navel and sternum just below your lower ribs. This chakra is associated with the digestive organs. It is the area where chi or life force is stored.

It's about your personal power and is associated with action, assertion, empowerment, and ego mastery. When the chakra is open and functioning as it should, you work well in a group setting, and feel in control. Malfunctions in the solar plexus chakra may leave you feeling passive, indecisive, withdrawn and powerless. Alternately, if the chakra is over-active, you might feel angry and exceedingly dominant in a group setting.

The solar plexus chakra is associated with the color yellow. Picture a vibrant, glowing sun in your solar plexus. Feel its warmth and energy.

Focus on this sun for a few moments. This sun represents your inner strength, your intuition, and all your inner resources. Allow your sun to glow brighter and stronger. You can hum the musical note E or Me.

M-E-D-I-T-A-T-E

FOURTH CHAKRA
Heart chakra, Anahata, love, compassion

Your fourth chakra is located at your heart, and is associated with the heart, lungs and circulatory system. This chakra channels love energy. A healthy heart chakra allows one to maintain a loving and compassionate perspective even in the most troubling situations.

Blockages can result in lack of compassion, immune system or heart problems. You might seem cold and distant to others. It's also about heartbreak, grief, pain, and fear of getting hurt. An over-active heart chakra can result in suffocating people with love, and acting solely in your self-interest.

Tune this powerful energy vortex by visualizing the color emerald green and feel yourself in a warm, loving, accepting environment. You might hum the musical note F or Fa.

M-E-D-I-T-A-T-E

FIFTH CHAKRA
Throat chakra, vishuddha, communication

Your throat chakra is associated with the vocal cords and the thyroid gland. It's the center for creativity and communication. The healthfulness of this chakra is signified by how openly and honestly a person expresses himself or herself. Falsehoods and half-truths energetically pollute the throat chakra. Unexpressed emotions also tend to constrict this energy center. Allow the truth of your inner voice to guide you.

You can tune your throat chakra by visualizing the color sky blue, focusing on the throat area, and maybe humming the musical note G or Sol.

M-E-D-I-T-A-T-E

SIXTH CHAKRA
Third eye chakra, Ajna, insight

Your third eye chakra, located in the center of your forehead, is related to your higher mental and intuitive abilities, the idea of looking forward. It is also associated with the pituitary gland, and it is responsible for providing a link between the inner and outer worlds. A healthy sixth chakra can ensure that you are on path and constantly finding support and valuable information through synchronicity, or meaningful coincidence, and psychic experiences. Blockages of the sixth chakra relate to delusions and fantasies.

Tune your sixth chakra by visualizing the color indigo, and possibly humming the musical note A or La.

M-E-D-I-T-A-T-E
SEVENTH CHAKRA
Crown chakra, sahasrara, spirituality

Located slightly above the top of your head, the crown chakra connects you with messages from higher realms. It's where you receive information about your life purpose and spiritual path. It's associated with the pineal gland and provides you with spiritual knowledge and understanding. It's about bliss.

You can tune your crown chakra by visualizing the color violet and you can hum the musical note "B" or "Ti". Visualize the violet light flowing through the crown chakra, through the third eye, through the throat chakra, through the heart chakra, through the solar plexus chakra, through the sacrum chakra, through the root chakra. As it flows down through the chakras from the Universal Life Force, it awakens and transforms.

Now feel love and joy flowing down through you, lighting your spine all the way to the root chakra, where it expands into a shimmering ball of light. Allow it to flow through you, allow yourself to really feel it.

M-E-D-I-T-A-T-E

Seed Mantras for Chakras

Here's another chakra meditation that focuses on bijas or seed mantras (see Chapter 5). Chakras bijas are gender-neutral and are associated with a symbol or shape instead of a god or goddess. By visualizing the image as well as repeating the one syllable mantra, you connect deeply with the chakra. The bijas also help activate the chakras, stimulating healing energy.

Select one of the following bijas for your next meditation. Say it over and over to yourself or aloud.

Lam (lahm) —root chakra, ruled by Earth, 'survival'

The seed sound for *muladhara* chakra has the quality of smell. By meditating on Lam, you might notice a mystical scent. While repeating the sound, visualize a square at the base of the spine. Chanting Lam while meditating on the root chakra helps you with issues related to patience, structure, stability, security, ability to manifest your dreams.

Vam (vahm) — sacral chakra, ruled by water, 'creativity'

The seed sound for *swadhisthana* chakra, located has the quality of taste. Visualize a circular shape a few inches below the naval as you recite the mantra. While repeating this bija, you're working with issues of wellness and well-being, sexuality, sensuality, pleasure, and abundance.

Ram (rahm)—solar plexus chakra, ruled by fire, 'strength'

The seed sound for the manipura chakra, ram has the quality of form. Visualize a triangular shape at the solar plexus. While chanting this bija, you're dealing with issues related to self-worth, self-esteem, confidence, personal power, freedom of choice.

Yam (yahm) — heart chakra, ruled by air, 'being open'

The seed sound for the *anahata* chakra, its quality is touch. Visualize a six-pointed star in the heart chakra. As you meditate, you might hear music or divinely inspired voices. By meditating on this chakra as you repeat the bija, you allow love to become the center of your life. You follow your heart's desires. You learn to love yourself as well as others. You learn to forgive, and open yourself to receive.

Ham (hoom)— throat chakra, ruled by sound, 'communication'

The seed sound for the *vishuddha* chakra, its quality is sound. Visualize a crescent shape in the throat chakra. Meditating on this is said to heal throat problems and aid in learning languages. Chanting this bija addresses will power, ability to express oneself, creativity, truthfulness, integrity.

Aum (ah-oh-mm)—third eye chakra, ruled by light, 'intuition'

The seed sound for the *ajna* chakra relates to self-reflection. Visualize a circle with two petals on either side. Meditating on this chakra allows you to see the big picture as well as develop psychic abilities. It's about wisdom, imagination, intuition, knowledge.

Aum (ah-oh-mm)—crown chakra, ruled by the principal of unity, 'connection with spirituality'

The seed sound for the *sahasrara* chakra, relates to cosmic intelligence. Visualize a spiral, circulating endlessly inward. Meditating on this chakra allows you to connect to a place outside of time and space, a place of wisdom, higher knowledge, bliss.

Chakras and Color Meditation

The following meditation uses chakras and their colors and is intended to relax, revitalize, and uplift. This meditation is also combined with visualization and leads to a spiritual quest.

Make yourself comfortable, and begin breathing deeply to the count of five. Relax your muscles from head to foot. When you are completely at ease, feel your body becoming lighter, almost weightless.

Picture a pure white glowing light directly in front of you. Concentrate on drawing the energy from this brilliant light into your body. Starting at your feet, feel it move slowly upward. As it moves up your legs, it turns to a pinkish color. When it reaches your upper thighs, it becomes a glowing red.

Red

Picture a flower bud at the lower end of your spine. Focus the red light on the flower, making it open petal by petal until it's in full bloom. Become aware of the warmth and tingling in your lower body.

Orange

Move the light upward, watching it turn from red to orange as it centers in your umbilical area. Once again picture the bud of a flower. Now open it with the orange energy force. See it in full bloom.

Yellow

When the flower is completely open and you feel the warmth, move the light upward to the solar plexus. There it turns to a bright yellow, like sunshine. Image another flower bud and watch it open. Drink in the sensations as it blossoms.

Green

Continue moving the light slowly upward. It turns from yellow to green as it reaches the area of the heart. Imagine the flower bud opening within the light. When you feel a sense of vitality, draw the light upward.

Blue

Watch as it turns to a pale blue by the time it reaches the throat area. Visualize the bud again. Open it, and feel the results. Any constriction in the throat is released. You are relaxed and at peace.

Purple

Now the light rises to the center of your forehead, where it becomes a deep indigo, and another bud blossoms in the intense light. Watch it open, petal by petal, and feel a tingling. In the center of the flower, imagine a closed eye. See this eye open. As it does, become aware of the brightness and clarity of the energy.

Violet

Finally, envision the light moving to the top of your head, changing to violet. Picture the bud of a flower once again, and watch each petal slowly open. As it does, you realize your entire body is enveloped in a luminous egg.

Being of Light

Now, feel yourself rising, passing through the ceiling and the roof, floating upward through the clouds. Picture a large golden door in front of you. The door is sectioned in panels, and on each one is a painting. Step closer to the door and examine the panels. Each one is a mandala, a symbol of wholeness. Reach out and touch them. As you are doing this, the door slowly opens and you enter.

You see a vast, bright space before you. And as you adjust to the brightness, you become aware of a benevolent presence, a being of light. Feel the love radiating from this being. You might think of this entity as a guide, an evolved master, or your higher self. Reach out and let the love enfold you.

Now see this presence in human form. Gaze into the being's eyes. Feel the sense of heightened awareness and joy. After a few minutes, thank the entity for all that you have experienced.

Finally, return slowly, taking with you an uplifting sense of well-being. You are totally relaxed, revitalized, and at one with your surroundings. Open your eyes. You are back.

Now you're ready to pursue the directed meditations.

PART TWO
EXPLORING THE JEWEL

CHAPTER 10

Directed Meditations

"Thirst for happiness being eternal, desires are without beginning."
—*The Yoga Sutras*, Patanjali

If there were an 800 number for complaints about meditation, no doubt most calls would come from people who can't quiet their minds. 'Busy-mind syndrome' is the main reason beginning meditators quit meditating. They get frustrated. I recall one student who took two classes from me and decided meditation was some kind of hoax, that it was impossible to quiet your mind. Since she couldn't quiet her mind, she assumed no one else could, either.

Because of such frustrations, I spend quite a bit of time working with visualization and inquiry to provide direction for meditations. In other words, I teach directed meditation, aimed at focusing on an intention, a desire, a dream, a goal. Not only does it give the mind something to focus on, but it can help resolve issues that are affecting your life. These can be large issues about the direction of your life or minor blockages that need to be overcome.

In fact, I used directed meditation when I faced a blockage about how to write this chapter. I knew I wanted to present a number of topics, such as abundance, breaking blockages, healing, and more. I would include affirmations for each one as the entry point to the meditation, and finish with a chant. But I wasn't certain how I was going to do the meditations.

Initially, I thought I would write separate meditations for each one. But I soon realized that might result in a considerable amount of repetition of material. Sitting at my desk I focused on my problem, seeking a solution. I affirmed that I would find the right approach and break through. Within a short time, I drifted into the alpha state where images and messages appear.

Often times, answer appears symbolically, and you need to interpret what you are experiencing in your meditation. I saw the singer-actress Cher. Immediately, I asked myself what she was doing in my meditation. I had not seen or heard anything about her in quite a while, long enough to know that I wasn't simply re-hashing something that I'd seen or heard recently.

I realized her name provided the answer. It was a pun. The answer was not Cher, but *share!* I needed to write meditations in a way that could be shared with any of the desires or issues. So that's what I did.

But are goal-oriented meditations that include affirmations and visualization really what meditation is about?

Non-Attachment

Maybe you've heard about meditation teachers who say visualization is just another way of thinking, that it's not true meditation. I've heard that, too, many times. Those same teachers might tell you to focus on letting go of attachments and seeking a state of nothingness. If you try that, you might find yourself floating in a void during your meditation. That can be pleasant, but it's actually another form of visualization—visualizing nothing.

Buddhists are great promoters of non-attachment. It's one of the central themes of the religion. That's fine if your focus is on detaching yourself from obsessive behavior related to people or things. But how far do you take that concept? Being non-attached to your children, for example, is probably a bad idea, one that could cause you to lose your children. In other words, there's a fine line between being non-attached and uncaring.

Some Buddhists say that happiness is not a viable goal of meditation, that happiness is a passing condition and an attachment. But so is unhappiness, and it seems there are plenty of unhappy Buddhists, weary of the world and all of its everyday attachments. As a result, casual observers tend to profile the Zen crowd as meditators who look on the world with a scowl and a sense of disgust about anything that hints of attachments. Insiders, however, will tell you that they are not unhappy. It's just that they don't ignore painful matters. In fact, they feel the way to deal with pain and difficulties is by focusing on such issues rather than running away from them.

My perspective is that it's better to meditate on what you want, imagining that you already have it, than to focus on what's lacking in your life. That only attracts more of the same. Sure, being preoccupied with material goods can drag us down and divert us from our spiritual quest. But having a dream, seeking abundance and other positive goals through visualization and affirmations should never be considered detrimental.

Wealth and prosperity are states of mind that are usually augured by money. Yes, money allows us to accumulate stuff, and possessing more objects is *not* a sure-fire pathway to inner peace and happiness. Certainly, there are people with lots of money who are unhappy, and there are people who misuse money and look only to possessions for meaning in their lives.

Of course, there are plenty of people without money who are bitterly unhappy. But happiness comes from within, not from the size of your bank account or the number of toys in your possession. Abundance is more than financial security. It's about living in the present moment and experiencing life to its fullest. After all, we are here in the physical world to feel and experience. If we think of ourselves essentially as spirits engaged in physical existence, then we can engage in life with a renewed interest and learn from our experiences, all the while knowing that it's transitory and our true home is the spirit realm.

I'm all for releasing attachments, such as negative emotional patterns that hold us back. But there's also value in pursuing *goals* through directed meditations. They not only provide structure that many beginning meditators need, but they work.

However, before we move into the directed meditations, let's briefly explore a meditation about true non-attachment. Our typical idea of non-attachment might be giving away all your possessions, leaving your home and family, maybe keeping a robe, sandals and a begging bowl. This is possible, though not prudent, especially in the Western World. True non-attachment, while impossible in the physical world, can be explored in meditation. Here's how:

Letting Go

Move into a comfortable position and take a few deep breaths. Scan your body, relaxing as you go. Settle in, slowing your breath.

Now start to let go of your identity. Begin with your name. Let it go. Imagine not having a name, or any role. Let go of all of your titles and roles: ie. mother, father, son, daughter, your career or job title, your qualifications, your history. Let it all go.

Let go of your religion, your race and nationality. Let go of your language. Let go of your gender. Let go of your body. How does it feel to be neither male or female. No name, gender, role, title, race, nationality, language. No body, merely a spark of awareness, exploring the unknown, touching upon the unknowable.

How do you feel? You're free, peaceful, immortal and eternal. You're connecting to your original self, linked to your creator, merging with higher awareness.

M-E-D-I-T-A-T-E

That's true non-attachment. It's worth exploring those ideas and feelings so you can face any fears of the unknown, of losing all that you are. In doing so, you connect with your deeper, eternal self, where you recognize that your physical life is but a blip. Yet, it's an important one, where you face challenges and opportunities to expand your awareness.

Working from Within

Everything that happens in life begins internally and is manifested externally. That might not seem to be the case when things don't go your way, but a closer examination of your thoughts might reveal stuff that you don't want to recognize. For example, a friend had money stolen from a checking account and two weeks later more money was stolen from another account in another bank. After the second incident, she calmed herself and meditated, looking deeply into her life.

She realized the loss of money was symbolic of the haphazard way she dealt with her finances. Although she had a steady income, she repeatedly was charged late fees on credit cards, which meant increased interest rates and a terrible credit rating. When she tried to get a loan for a new car, her application was rejected. She knew it was time to make a change. She reorganized her finances, merging her debt, and cutting up excessive credit cards. After she did so, she was pleased to find out the banks were reimbursing her on the stolen money.

The theft of funds from her accounts had angered and frightened her. But ultimately with the help of meditation, she took steps to improve her finances, and the lost money came back to her.

While meditation is a valuable tool for relieving stress, becoming more centered, aware and mindful, we can fine-tune our meditations to meet our needs and desires. The deeper you go, the more likely you are to achieve positive results. The following directed meditations, therefore, are enhanced with affirmations and chants.

Making Your Choices

Choose a topic for meditation, an important issue, something you desire in your life. Next, select a related affirmation. Work with it. Say it to yourself with conviction, repeating it several times. Associate it with the specifics of your issue, but focus on the solution, not the problem. You might write it long-hand or on your computer several times before you begin the meditation. Later, you can repeat the affirmation over and over during the day, visualizing the desired results.

As you say your affirmations, imagine that whatever you desire has already happened. Notice how it feels, how happy you are, how you look.

You can pick different affirmations from the choices each time that you work with the meditation. As you move into the meditation, allow yourself at least fifteen minutes. Think of it as enjoyable and relaxing as you visualize and create your new self.

Chanting

At the end of your meditation, you can return to your affirmation and turn it into a chant. You do so by repeating it aloud 108 times, keeping track on your fingers or with mala beads, which conveniently have 108 beads. Alternately, you can say the chant aloud for two minutes, whisper it for two minutes, and say it to yourself for two minutes. Gradually, you can expand to three minutes each. By chanting your affirmation, you are sealing the message. When you're done, release it, let it go, and move on with your day.

As you experiment with directed meditations, you can use this format to expand into other areas of personal concern, and create your own related affirmations.

Your Desire

Abundance

What is it that's keeping you from leading a life filled with abundance? Is it a fear that wealth would change your life in adverse ways? Is it a concern that having money isn't spiritual? Or, that you don't deserve wealth?

Think of money as energy without giving it a positive or negative value. Let go of any unfavorable thoughts or impressions you have about people who are rich. Equate abundance with happiness, kindness and generosity. Add emotion to the equation. You really want this, right? How does it feel to have all the money you need and more? With practice, your new concept of wealth and prosperity will filter into all aspects of your life.

As you move into the relaxation, imagine everything that you need is flowing into your life. Express gratitude for what are receiving. Take your time and allow the relaxation process to align you for your meditation. But first find an affirmation that works for you.

Affirmations
- Prosperity surrounds me, prosperity flows through my life.
- Wonderful things are unfolding for me.
- I take advantage of new opportunities.
- There is abundance in the universe for every living being.

- I am open and receptive to new avenues of income.
- I effortlessly attract all the wealth I desire.
- I sense a natural attraction to wealth and comforts.
- I embrace prosperity in all of its forms.
- I am happy, healthy and prosperous.
- All that I touch turns to gold. Thank you, thank you, thank you!
- I now create a wonderful new job.

Breaking Blockages

Are you feeling stressed and stuck, unable to move ahead? Do you seem to repeat the same mistakes and get frustrated? We all experience blockages at times. The key is to move beyond these seemingly difficult barriers before they become a new normal and affect your well being—physical, emotional, mental and spiritual. It takes strong desire, courage and confidence, and a heart-felt willingness to change and break through the blockages.

Affirmations
- All that blocks me from moving ahead and achieving my goals fades away.
- I'm drawing on my strength and inner light to remove all blockages.
- Wonderful things are unfolding for me. All blockages are removed.
- Help and guidance come my way.
- Everything unfolds as it should.

Finding Your Path in Life

Do you feel as if you're only working to meet your needs and not fulfilling your purpose in life? Maybe you know there's something more you should be doing, but you're having difficulty defining your higher purpose. If that's the case, you need to focus on some basic questions. Who are you and what do you really want?

Affirmations
- My purpose is now clear and I'm ready to fulfill it.
- I'm moving ahead in my life. I know my direction now.
- I'm confident I can find my way. I'm on my path.
- My life plan is on schedule. I'm right where I'm supposed to be.
- I'm empowered to life my life blissfully.
- I love and approve of myself and know I will make the right decisions.

Meeting Your Soul Mate

Begin by accepting—if you haven't already—the concept that everyone has a soul mate and you can find that person. Believe that you not only deserve to find that special person, but you have an innate ability to do so. Positive affirmations will help you radiate a positive energy that can attract your soul mate to you.

Imagine what the person might look like. What is his or her temperament? Is he or she a spiritual person? Include all the qualities that you are looking for in that right person. As you say one of the following affirmations, imagine that you are already in touch with that special person.

Affirmations
- My mind and heart are attracting my soul mate.
- I know I am already connecting with my soul mate.
- I radiate a loving and inviting energy.
- My soul mate is attracted to me.
- My soul mate and I are destined for each other.
- I deserve to find my soul mate now.
- My soul mate and I are meant to be together.
- I am thankful for all the love in my life.

Self-Healing

Self-healing is all about loving yourself, loving life, and everyone who comes into your life or passes through it. Healing yourself begins with the mind. It requires overcoming any negative programming that might have caused self-loathing. That attitude leads to subconsciously punishing yourself by attracting illness, often through detrimental behavior, such as excessive alcohol consumption, a poor diet, or a shortage of sleep.

Healing affirmations can help overcome the thoughts and actions that lead to illness. Thinking and worrying about illness doesn't help. Even when you're not feeling well, it's important to find something to feel positive about.

Healthy thoughts can create a healthy body, and that's where healing affirmations, meditation and visualization come into play. When you recognize that you have a right to be a healthy and happy human being, you will have an excellent chance at achieving your full potential.

Affirmations
- I'm happy and grateful to be healthy again.
- My medication is gratitude and positive thinking.
- Every day in every way I'm getting healthier and healthier.
- I sleep well and wake up fresh.
- I eat healthy and stay healthy.
- Every cell in my body radiates health.
- I exercise on a regular basis and enjoy it.
- I am grateful for my healthy body.
- I feel great and look great.
- I am free of pain and full of energy.
- I radiate health, love and compassion.

Intuitive Guidance

You can improve your life dramatically by paying attention to the intuitive nudges that come your way. When you're puzzling over something or attempting to make a decision, you might suddenly experience a synchronicity, or meaningful coincidence, that offers you a new perspective. Signs and symbols, messages from dreams, and hunches are other ways that you draw on your intuitive nature to give you an edge on whatever you're doing or attempting.

An impulse to do or try something that isn't part of your daily routine can also be the voice of your intuitive self as it nudges you in a new direction, to break away from old patterns. So rather than stifling an impulse or telling yourself you don't have the time or energy to do it, follow the impulse. See where it leads you.

Affirmations
- I notice synchronicity or meaningful coincidences often and they guide me.
- I am one with the universe and at peace with myself.
- I received wisdom and guidance from ancestors and higher beings.
- I am protected and guided.
- I find guidance through dreams and meditation.

Overcoming Negativity

If your thoughts are draining you emotionally, meditation combined with positive affirmations are an excellent way to get you moving ahead into a healthy and productive lifestyle. Affirmations can free you from your dependence on other people's opinions, attitudes, or feelings about you. They can help you feel good about yourself, and overcome any negativity.

You can also overcome negative feelings from the past and face the present with a clear view. In doing so, you give yourself permission to grow and change, to take risks, improve your well-being, and create a better life.

Affirmations
- I remain confident and unaffected by negativity around me.
- I am competent and energetic, strong and enthusiastic.
- I am loving, caring and courageous.
- Good things are happening for me.
- I'm trusting and forgiving.
- I'm intelligent, confident and relaxed.
- I face my fears and overcome them.
- I am joyful and appreciative.

Enhancing Creativity

There's no such thing as a non-creative person, only people who haven't pursued their own innate talents. Creativity is not just about an ability to paint a picture or write a story. It's a spark within you that allows you to come up with new ideas or present ideas in new ways. It's about inspiration. It's about changing a black and white portrait of reality into a colorful one. Creativity is entertaining; creativity is functional.

Affirmations
- I possess an endless supply of creative energy.
- Being creative makes me feel so alive.
- I gratefully accept all the creative ideas that flow my way.
- I am creative and open to new opportunities.
- I am talented and willing to share my knowledge.
- I am open to taking a risk.
- I challenge myself to try a new approach.
- Creative inspiration follows me wherever I go.
- I follow where my inspiration leads.

Once you've selected your desire and your affirmation, you can choose one of the directed meditations below. It's a good idea to start by relaxing from head to toe. As mentioned earlier, after your meditation, you can turn your affirmation into a chant, sealing the deal, so to speak.

Relaxing

Here's a quick method that will work with any of the meditations.
Get comfortable.
Take several deep breaths. Breathe in relaxation, exhale tension. Feel yourself relaxing more and more with each exhalation.
Slow your breath and focus on the top of your head, your forehead, your cheeks and jaw. Feel your face relaxing.
Feel all the muscles in your neck relax, and feel the relaxation flowing over your shoulders and down your arms to your wrists and hands. Feel the tension draining out your fingertips.

Take another deep breath, filling your lungs, and as you exhale, let your chest and upper back relax, then your middle and lower back. Breathe in and out as you let your abdominal muscles relax.

Relax your hips, pelvic area and buttocks, your thighs and knees. Relax your lower legs, your ankles and feet. Inhale relaxation and exhale tension, letting it drain out the bottom of your feet.

Let your internal organs relax, and let your mind relax. Take your time and let the relaxation process take you deeper.

Now you're ready to move on to one of the directed meditations.

The Golden Light Meditation

Take three deep breaths, shift to gentle breathing. Connect with the Earth through your feet. Feel your roots going deeper and deeper into the Earth, communing with the heart of Mother Earth. Feel yourself becoming more and more receptive. Now that you are open to receiving, see yourself walking through a vast field of gold flowers under a bright sunlit sky. The flowers represent the *(YOUR TOPIC)* that is coming your way.

You come to a circular opening in the middle of the field, where you lay down and soak in the sun's transforming energy. Feel the warmth and allow the sun's energy to pour into you, empowering you, opening new opportunities for *(YOUR TOPIC)*.

Gradually, you realize that you are engulfed in a glowing, golden capsule of light. It surrounds you and fills you. The golden light expands and spreads throughout the circle forming a glowing dome of energy. Inhale that energy, pulling in *(YOUR TOPIC)*. Exhale and relax more deeply. Hold the image for a couple of minutes, soaking in the shimmering gold light.

The dome of light begins to shrink around you again. It intensifies and forms a glowing golden ball at the heart chakra. Now specify what it is you desire. Imagine it is yours, and visualize yourself right in the center of the golden ball of light. How do you feel? How do you look? See it there and know that it is yours. Know that what you seek is appropriate for you, that you deserve it. Let go of any limiting beliefs that might be holding you back. Inhale and exhale.

Feel the joy and happiness. Know that what you're receiving is beneficial and causes no harm to others. It provides opportunities for you to share your joy. Breath deeply, inhaling, exhaling. Then calm your breath.

Now the golden ball of light slowly rises to your throat chakra, your third eye or brow chakra, the crown chakra, and it continues to rise higher and higher melding with a luminous being—your higher self or spirit guide—who absorbs it. You release it, letting it go and knowing that your desires will be fulfilled.

Allow your heart chakra to close now, locking in your desire. As you complete your meditation, give thanks for what you have already received and what you will receive. Recognize that gratitude is a powerful emotion that attracts whatever you desire. Take another deep breath and exhale, knowing that you are ready to achieve *(YOUR TOPIC)*.

Meditate for at least 15 minutes.

M-E-D-I-T-A-T-E

The Star Meditation

This meditation was introduced to me years ago in a workshop by John Perkins, author of *The World Is As You Dream it* and other books. The meditation provides an excellent means to destroy the barriers keeping you from completing a task or goal, following a dream, or finding a dream. Like the first meditation, you can apply it to any issue, including attaining abundance, a creative break-through, self-healing, overcoming negativity, others of your choice.

Begin by focusing on your issue. Think about it awhile and repeat your affirmation to yourself. Think of it as your new reality. Gradually, let go of your thoughts, shut your eyes, and focus on the field of darkness in front of you. Notice a point of light forming in the distance. Slowly, it begins to grow and intensify. Watch it expand into a brilliant silver star that fills the entire field of your vision.

Now move the bright star to the crown of your head, or the crown chakra-- *sahasrara* (SAW-HAS-RA). See and feel its energy growing more and more intense as it continues to expand. Then, suddenly, when it can't intensify any further, the star explodes and destroys the barriers blocking your way.

Now see the star forming *again* at the crown chakra. The energy intensifies as the star expands and expands, then bursts with a release of incredible energy. The blockages are blown away. Repeat the process one more time.

Next, move the silver star to your heart chakra or fourth chakra, *anahata*. See and feel the energy intensifying as the star glows and grows. It continues to grow larger and hotter until the energy explodes, smashing the barriers obstructing your way. Again, see the star re-forming at your heart. It becomes brighter and brighter, glowing with a new intensity. It expands and expands and once again, see and feel the star exploding and wiping away everything that blocks you from achieving your dream or your goal, or resolving your issue. Repeat the process one more time.

Now move the silver star to a point between your navel and groin, the second chakra. Known as *svadhisthana*, the second chakra is the center of physical, sexual, and creative energy. See the star's heat intensifying. See it becoming brighter and brighter as it expands and expands even further. See it explode, sending forth its energy and annihilating all the barriers.

Watch again as the silver star re-forms at the second chakra and swells and brightens until you can see nothing but its brightness, and then feel it erupt and blast apart, removing all obstacles from your path. Repeat the sequence one more time.

Finally, see the star re-forming directly in front of you, filling your vision. Watch as it gradually shrinks away to a point, then vanishes altogether. Open your eyes slightly again and sit quietly. Your eyelids are heavy and you are staring at a point somewhere out in front of you. Know that the power you have released has obliterated the blocks holding you back from your new reality. Express your gratitude.

Remain seated in silence for a couple of minutes, then you can begin chanting your affirmation.

Crystal Cavern Meditation

Like the two other directed meditations, visualization will play a key role in guiding you. After you've relaxed, begin by imagining that you're following a trail in a park-like setting on a pleasant day.

Gradually, you come to steps that lead up a hill. At the top, you reach a heavy wooden door with a rounded top that's built into the side of the hill. As you slowly approach it, the door creaks open, and you see a shadowy tunnel.

Cautiously, you step inside and notice a light in the distance. You don't feel any fear. In fact, you sense that something interesting awaits you. You move ahead through the cool air, toward the illumination. With each step, you feel lighter and lighter until you are almost gliding along.

You stop as you come to an enormous cavern—a crystal cavern with bright, glittering walls, ceiling, and floor. Everything is crystal, and you feel a high energy streaming through you.

Then you see a mirror like no other, and you move closer. You can see yourself, and into yourself. You see your hope and dreams clearly. Maybe there's something you're doing and don't want to be doing or something you wish you were doing, but aren't.

Know that this chamber magnifies the laws of attraction. It's much easier here for your inner desires to connect with outer experiences.

Look closely in the mirror at yourself, and find your desire. Know that you can obtain it, that it is within your reach. See yourself with it and notice how you feel. Then release the image. Pay attention to your breath for a minute or two before continuing.

When you're ready, look closely at yourself again and either focus on your desire, or find something else about yourself and your life that's missing. Know that you can obtain it. How do you feel? How do you look now that you have it? Then, release the image. Focus on your breath again.

When you're ready, look in the mirror one more time, and repeat the process. Find a new desire or work with the most important one.

After you've released the image this time, see your entire body surrounded by energy, below you, above you, all around you. Notice this energy coming in and around you and flowing upward from your feet, your legs, your torso, and through your head. Know that your desire, your wishes and dreams will come true.

Now feel yourself lifting up with the energy and leaving the crystal cavern right through the roof. Go with the flow. Feel yourself becoming aligned with the energy, moving with it. And you're back.

Chant

After your meditation, return to your affirmation, but now as you repeat it aloud over and over, it becomes a chant. At first, it may seem you are just saying the words, but gradually the words become a mantra, and instead of saying them, you are chanting.

To enhance your affirmation, you can add one of the bija mantras at the end of each repetition. Here's a list of powerful bijas that work well with affirmations.

Shrim [shreem]: The seed sound for abundance and prosperity.

Gum [gum]: The masculine seed sound linked to Ganaesha, the remover of obstacles who opens the doors to success in your endeavors.

Dum [doom]: A mantra for protection and overcoming fears.

Eim [I'm]: The seed sound for success in attracting spiritual knowledge.

Krim [kreem]: feminine energy and can be called upon when you're intent on building power.

Klim [kleem]: The seed sound for attraction of what you desire.

Kshraum [ksh-roum]: The seed sound for getting rid of on-going negative situations.

In the next chapter, we move from directed meditations to an exploration of *siddhis,* or psychic power.

CHAPTER 11

Psi & the Siddhi

"It is my personal opinion that in the science of the future reality will neither be 'psychic' nor 'physical' but somehow both and somehow neither."
—Wolfgang Pauli

In yoga philosophy, *siddhis* are the super-mind stuff of advanced yogis and meditators. They're about psi, or psychic functioning: telepathy, precognition, clairvoyance, psycho-kinesis, and other aspects of the paranormal.

While mainstream Western science lumps such topics into the realm of fantasy and superstition, most of us accept the reality of telepathy and other forms of extra sensory perception. We've not only heard stories from reliable sources, but we've had one, or possibly many, psychic experiences.

Through your practice of meditation, your intuitive abilities could expand and more stuff could happen. By meditating on a regular basis, you become more mindful of your thoughts, and you'll notice things that you previously might've overlooked. So what are these things, you might ask, and do you really want to know about them?

Synchronicity

Let's say you just picked up this book and wondered if it included anything about meditation and psychic abilities. You opened it at random and here you are. You turned right to the chapter on that very topic. What a coincidence, right? If it's meaningful to you, and it probably would be, since this is what you were looking for, then it's a synchronicity.

Simply put, a synchronicity occurs when similar inner and outer experiences come together without the help of cause and effect and it's meaningful to the observer. In the example above, your thought was the inner experience and the random page you turned to was the outer experience. There was no cause and effect, because you didn't look at the table of contents to lead you logically to a possible answer to your question.

But what does it mean? That's always what people ask. In this case, it might mean you're on the right path, exploring the right question. If you had randomly turned to another page, you might've found something else of interest and ended or delayed your quest to explore the link between meditation and psychic abilities. It's like the saying: Wherever you go, there you are. And, for the moment, here you are.

Here's another question that might've just occurred to you: What is the relationship between synchronicity and psychic abilities? Glad you asked. Synchronicity is like an umbrella covering all aspects of psychic phenomena that I mentioned above. That concept of synchronicity is attributed to the famed psychotherapist Carl Jung, who coined the term.

Jung, of course, didn't create meaningful coincidence. But he was the researcher who highlighted its importance and designated it as the overall theme of paranormal phenomena. He did so because such experiences meet the criteria for synchronicity. Say that you happened to think about an old friend with whom you had lost contact years ago. You click onto Facebook a while later and *bingo!* That person had just sent you a friend request.

You're startled and impressed. Wow, you're psychic. You just had a telepathic experience. Or maybe it was precognitive. Either way, it's also synchronicity because it involved similar inner and outer events coming together that didn't require cause and effect, and it was a meaningful experience.

Synchronicity and Mindfulness

During your next meditation, ask for guidance on a matter of importance to you. Maybe it relates to a possible career move or a relationship issue. Give yourself the suggestion that in the next twenty-four hours, you will experience a meaningful coincidence that will nudge you in the right direction.

Maybe something will come to you immediately. For example, your meditation is interrupted by a phone call, and it turns out that the person calling provided you with just what you needed. Synchronicity!

Sometimes synchronicities are not so obvious. Remain mindful during your day so you don't miss any subtle hints.

Yoga Sutras

In yoga philosophy, paranormal abilities, as mentioned earlier, are referred to as siddhis, a Sanskrit word meaning perfection. The historic document that explains siddhis is called *The Yoga Sutras* and was a written version of a collection of oral teachings that had been handed down through countless generations. The *Yoga Sutras* were assembled in writing about 2,000 years ago by a sage and scribe named Patanjali. They include four books consisting of 196 sutras or aphorisms. The third book, called *Vibhuti Pada,* describes the siddhis in 56 sutras.

Patanjali considered the siddhis natural side-effects of deep meditation when the meditator can maintain a refined state of mind known as *samyama*. He cautioned not to think of siddhis as supernormal. That could result in too much emphasis on the ego and deter you from advancing in your spiritual quest. For that reason, Patanjali and many other sages have downplayed the importance of pursuing the siddhis.

In spite of his cautionary approach, Patanjali included more than two dozen siddhis that can be categorized as either exceptional mind-body control, clairvoyance, or psycho-kinesis. Most of these abilities relate to clairvoyance, the ability to gain knowledge about something taking place at a distance or beyond the normal senses.

Some of the siddhis actually sound like abilities found in fantasy novels, movies or television shows about super heroes or villains. Among them are the ability to become invisible, to change one's appearance or size, to levitate or walk on water, to influence others to act in accordance with your will, to withstand extremely cold temperatures without clothing and to preserve your body from decay after death. Heady stuff. Even after death.

Let's take a closer look at the siddis. Here they are, as divided in the *Vibhuti Pada:*

The Eight Primary Siddhis

- *Anima Siddhi:* The ability to decrease the size of your body so that you are able to be smaller than a subatomic energy particle. You can move through objects.
- *Mahima Siddhi:* The ability to increase the size of your body so that you ultimately can become as large as the universe.
- *Laghima Siddhi:* The ability to become as light as air and fly at will.
- *Prapti Siddhi:* The ability to manifest any object into the palm of your hand.
- *Prakamya Siddhi:* The ability to obtain anything you desire.
- *Ishita Siddhi:* The ability to seemingly defy the laws of nature and perform astonishing tasks such as walking on water or breathing fire.
- *Vashita Siddhi:* The ability to control what other people do.
- *Kamavasayita Siddhi:* The ability to do anything you desire. This is the highest of the eight and contains most of the abilities of the other siddhis.

Supposedly, only advanced practitioners can achieve the primary siddhis, and they rarely reveal their abilities.

The Ten Secondary Siddhis

1. The ability to be free from hunger and thirst, no longer dependent on food and water.
2. The ability to hear distant sounds and conversations. It's the same as the psychic ability known as clairaudience.
3. The ability to see distant events, also known as clairvoyance.
4. The ability to travel to any location instantly, ie. teleportation.
5. The ability to alter the size of one's physical body at will.
6. The ability to enter anyone's body and partake in their senses.

7. The ability to control the time of one's death.
8. The ability to observe the activities of beings in other realms or dimensions.
9. The ability to make anything happen that you wish.
10. The ability to create reality through your spoken words.

Supposedly, many people can experience these secondary siddhis in the natural course of their spiritual growth. Even though the last five are called inferior, they're still pretty awesome.

The Five Inferior Siddhis

- The ability to know the future, present and past.
- The ability to tolerate heat and cold.
- The ability to know what others are thinking.
- The ability to stop the effects of water, fire and poison.
- The ability to avoid being conquered by others.

So how do these astonishing powers stack up with science? Is there really a connection between meditation and such supernormal abilities, or is it part of a mythology from the distant past?

Psi and Science

Scientists who study the paranormal don't get much respect in mainstream science circles. Yet, some bold researchers have set out to test Patanjali's assertions that meditation increases the occurrence of siddhis, or psychic experiences. Research from the 1970s to the mid-1990s, including 16 studies, suggests that a regular meditation practice does improve psychic abilities.

Researcher Gertrude Schmeidler analyzed the results and concluded in a journal article that "meditation is conducive to ESP (extra sensory perception) success if (and only if) the meditators wholeheartedly accept the experimental procedure and the goal of the research." Schmeidler's conditional acceptance illuminated the problem that psi abilities and meditation don't always mix in a sterile laboratory environment.

Parapsychologist Dean Radin in his book, *SUPERNORMAL:*

Science, Yoga and the Evidence for Extraordinary Psychic Abilities, writes: "From a scientific perspective, the mere *existence* of these phenomena, regardless of how weak or unreliable they may be, is astonishing. It tells us that the modern understanding of the human mind, which is based on the neurosciences and its approach to studying brain functions, has completely overlooked a fundamental aspect of our capacity and potentials."

More recently, British psychologist Serena Roney-Dougal studied Tibetan Buddhist meditators in northeastern India with the intent to find out if increased levels of meditation result in increased psychic abilities. The participants relaxed for five minutes, then meditated for 15 minutes. Then they were asked to describe a photograph on Roney-Dougal's laptop computer, and sketch it. Afterwards, they were shown four photos on the computer and asked to select the photo that was closest to the image they saw in their vision.

A variation of the procedure tested meditators' abilities to see the future. They were asked to describe and draw a picture that would be randomly selected on the computer from a collection of twenty-five photos.

The result of the study revealed evidence that more experienced meditators performed at a higher level when it came to exhibiting psi abilities. When all the tests were compiled, the odds against chance were 8,500 to 1. While scientific studies of meditation have become popular and the results positive, mainstream researchers continue to shy away from studying the siddhis. It's almost as if they are saying, *If the siddhis exist, we don't want to know about it.*

Radin puts it this way: "The siddhis are a core component of most meditative traditions, so one would think that any serious research on this topic would *have* to include a discussion of the siddhis. But most haven't, and the abyss is especially conspicuous in the neurosciences, where merely mentioning this topic in a positive tone is strictly forbidden."

Developing Your Psi Factor

Even if you don't think you have any psychic abilities, the good news is that you probably do have some abilities and aren't aware of them, or you dismiss your psychic hits as mere coincidence. One of the best ways to enhance or develop your native skills is to meditate on a regular basis.

However, let's keep things in perspective. Traditional yoga-meditation practices, as I mentioned, de-emphasize the importance of developing siddhis. These abilities are considered side effects, not the goal of the practice. In other words, siddhis are a distraction that take us away from the path of spiritual enlightenment. That said, advanced yogis on the traditional path never doubt the existence of these abilities.

Not so in Western culture, where paranormal abilities are not only dismissed by mainstream science, but also looked upon with considerable suspicion by conservative branches of religions. But unless we explore these supposed abilities for ourselves, we are simply accepting the word of others, the so-called authorities. We wouldn't take other people's opinion as the only criteria for buying a certain make and model of car. So why do it when we're dealing with the nature of reality? One's own experiences are paramount in developing an accurate assessment of these abilities.

If you're interested in exploring your own talents through your meditation practice, several psychic development exercises follow, most adapted from my book *Psychic Power: Discovering Your Sixth Sense at Any Age*. However, if your goal is to do something awesome—take your pick from the list of siddhis—that will impress your friends, you're probably in for a surprise. The deeper you pursue these abilities, you'll probably find that your original intentions were, well, pretty superficial.

The surprise is that spiritual development seems to be an inevitable result of exploring the siddhis through meditation and related exercises. Granted, that's the opposite of what the yogi sages say, but it seems a more fitting approach for some of us. After all, there's more than one path to achieving a higher state of being, what the yogis call *Samadhi*, the height of divine consciousness.

Let's take a look at some of the most recognized forms of psychic abilities. The exercises follow the descriptions and examples.

Precognition

Is it possible to see future events? If so, can we alter the future?

Research shows that the answer to both questions is yes. We can and do get glimpses of probable future events, but the future is not predestined. If we know what might happen, we can change circumstances and shift our future reality. For example, there are numerous reports of people foreseeing disasters, such as airplane crashes, and changing their plans, thus saving their lives and altering their futures.

We all have the potential to glimpse future events. The reason these perceptions are rare for most of us, is that we get in the way of our abilities. Our busy minds block us, and so do our beliefs of what is real and what is possible. But sometimes a near-future event is so dramatic or earth-shaking that these impressions reach our conscious minds. One of the best examples are the numerous documented instances in which people had such a strong sense of foreboding that they didn't go to work at the Twin Towers on September 11, 2001. In addition, many others, especially in New York City, had dreams and premonitions of the world-changing disaster that was about to take place.

In the following series of exercises related to precognition, you can discover which inner sense—feeling, seeing, or hearings—works best for you. For each exercise, take several minutes to move into your meditative state.

Begin by relaxing with several deep breaths. Have a question you would like answered, preferably about something that is coming up in your life. Select a time frame, but don't go out past six months. The closer you target to the present, fewer variables come into play that could alter the veracity of your prediction.

Seeing the Future

Phrase your question in terms of vision, such as, "What do I see happening related to..." In a relaxed state, with your eyes closed, notice how your vision seems directed toward your brow or 'third eye.' Look for images to appear like a movie in your mind. Even if the images don't seem to relate to your question, don't dismiss them as meaningless. Look for anything symbolic, as if your vision was a dream, and see how you can interpret it.

Sensing the Future

With your question in mind, phrase it in terms of bodily sensations. In other words, "How do I feel about..." Become aware of the area between your solar plexus and your belly. What is your gut feeling about the matter?

Notice any sensations or emotions that you experience. Is it a feeling of joy or foreboding, anger or fear? Is it a positive or negative feeling? If you feel nothing, what kind of nothing is it? Does it indicate something hidden, a lack of something, or 'nothing good?' If what you perceive through your feelings is something you don't like, what can you do to change the circumstances?

Hearing the Future

Keeping your question in mind, relate it to hearing. For example, "What do I hear related to..." Relax and close your eyes. Filter out any outside sounds, such as traffic. Imagine a voice whispering a message. Look for ways to apply the answer to your question, even if it doesn't seem related.

Mind-to-Mind Communication

Throughout history, sending and receiving information by means of a sixth sense has been a professed ability for certain talented individuals and a spontaneous experience for many others. Anthropologists studying primitive cultures have observed members communicating over long distances through telepathy. Even today with our instantaneous means of electronic and digital communication systems, the ability to connect mind-to-mind still exists, as thousands of studies have shown.

Some of the first scientific experiments were conducted in the mid-nineteenth century and involved subjects who were hypnotized. In one experiment, a Scottish surgeon, James Esdaile, hypnotized and blindfolded a man who he knew was a viable subject because the man had undergone surgery with hypnosis as his only anesthesia. In this instance, Esdaile tried to telepathically send tastes and smells to the man, the receiver. With an assistant as an intermediary, Esdaile 'sampled' substances such as salt, brandy, and a lime. When the assistant tasted a partially rotten lime, the subject made a wry face and said, "I taste a nasty old lime." He was equally successful with the other substances.

Radin notes: "Telepathy tests developed over many decades have evolved into experiments that are as close to perfect as anyone has been able to devise so far. The results indicate that the likelihood that telepathy exists is as close to 'proven' as contemporary science can establish."

Receiving Images #1

You can test your own skills with these simple experiments, working with a friend. Keep in mind that the deeper you go into a meditative state, the more likely you are to be successful.

Before you begin, tell your friend to pick a fruit to send to you. She should visualize the fruit clearly: the color and shape, the texture and the taste. The friend should repeat the name of the fruit silently as she sends an image to you, but only after you indicate that you are ready to receive.

Move into your meditative state, taking several deep breaths as you clear your mind and relax. When you're ready, you might simply lift your hand to signal the sender to begin. Surprisingly, you might already be getting images before the test 'officially' begins. Notice which senses are strongest. Can you taste the fruit, see its color, notice how it feels? Don't spend more than a minute on the target, and don't worry if you think you are guessing or that it's just your imagination.

Try another target. Maybe add vegetables into the mix of your telepathic salad.

Receiving Images #2

Here's another test to try with a friend who acts as a sender. In this case, your friend will cut out ten photos from magazines. Preferably, the photos will be of scenery, buildings, and action shots rather than headshots. Make sure that you don't see them in advance. Have a notebook and pen or pencil handy.

When you're relaxed and focused, the sender should retreat to a separate room, select one of the photos and send it to you telepathically. Notice any fleeting images that come to mind. Either jot down what you see, so you won't forget, or quickly sketch the image.

After a couple of minutes, the sender should signal you, maybe by tapping on the wall or saying 'next,' then repeat the process with the second photo. The photos and your drawings and notes should be numbered. Afterwards, compare the photos with your responses.

'Clear Seeing'

Imagine that there was no sender in the above exercise and the photos were randomly selected by a computer program, automatically numbered and stored. If you could 'see' those photos in the same way that you attempted to see the ones sent by your friend, then you would be practicing clairvoyance, a French word that means 'clear seeing.'

The ability 'to see' objects hidden or distant from your normal vision, or even to see what's going on elsewhere, is also known as remote viewing. Clairsentience concerns feelings related to such a target and clairaudience is when hearing is the sense that picks up information about a target.

Serious scientific research into remote viewing, or clairvoyance, began in 1973 at the Stanford Research Institute in Menlo, California, under the direction of Harold Putoff and Russell Targ. The early experiments involved a highly sensitive psychic researcher and artist named Ingo Swann. At first, they asked Swann to describe objects that were placed in another room. But when Swann became bored with the repetitive tasks, he created a new challenge.

He asked Putoff and Targ to give him map coordinates and see if he could describe the location. One of the most interesting results occurred when a skeptical scientist submitted coordinates. This is what Swann said, according to the laboratory transcripts:

This seems to be some sort of mounds or rolling hills. There is a city to the north; I can see taller buildings and some smog. This seems to be a strange place, somewhat like the lawns one would find around a military base, but I get the impression that either there are some old bunkers around or maybe this is a covered reservoir. There must be a flagpole, some highways to the west, possibly a river over to the far east, to the south more city...There is something strange about this area, but since I don't know what to look for within the scope of the cloudy ability, it is extremely difficult to make decisions on what is there and what is not. Imagination seems to get in the way. For example, I get the impression of something underground, but I'm not sure.

Swann also drew a picture of the image he'd seen. The transcript and picture were mailed to the scientist, who called back upon receiving it. The target was an underground missile site, and the drawing was accurate, even to scale.

As a result of the success rate of the experiments at the Stanford Research Institute, the U.S. government started taking an interest in the research. By the late 1970s, the CIA and the U.S. Army began training psychics for spying, a program ultimately called Stargate. It lasted twenty years.

Probably the most talented and successful of the psychic spies was Joe McMoneagle. Known as Remote Viewer #001, he joined the program in 1978 and stayed with it until it ended in 1994. Typically, McMoneagle would meditate for up to forty-five minutes before he began remote viewing his target.

Jim Schnabel, author of *Remote Viewers: The Secret History of America's Psychic Spies,* relates how, in one instance, McMoneagle was given an envelope with a picture inside and was told only that it was a person. He was given several dates and times and asked to describe the person and his surroundings at each time. He proceeded to describe a man with dark hair and dressed in a business suit. He was driving a car through hilly countryside. About five minutes into the session, McMoneagle abruptly stopped and said he couldn't go any further. He said it was as if the picture of the man turned sideways and disappeared. He couldn't follow the man, he said, because he couldn't go where the man went.

Later, McMoneagle found out that the man in question was a foreign agent who had failed to appear at a meeting and disappeared. But the mystery was solved when it was learned that he died in a car accident. During the time frame that McMoneagle had used in his session, the man had driven his car over a cliff, while speeding along a winding road in Italy.

In 1999, I wrote *PSI/NET*, the first of two novels about remote viewing. Both were co-authored with actor Billy Dee Williams, who had hoped to play the lead role in a movie based on the first book. I asked McMoneagle to read the manuscript and he kindly provided a blurb for the book. Later, after meeting McMoneagle in person, I had the opportunity to personally test his remote viewing skills. I sealed a photograph inside an envelope and on the outside of it I wrote, "Target BG5406," and the simple directions, *Describe purpose of target*. The letters and numbers held no significance and were simply a focus-point for McMoneagle.

After meditating, he described a collection of small single-level buildings. "There is a very exotic ground-plane system and electronic frequency-tuning system involved here, as well as some sort of a sophisticated monitoring system emplaced which is in twenty-four-hour operation. I'm also getting a very strong sensitivity feeling...not sensitive in the sense of electronics, but sensitive in the sense of security. These systems are associated with Special Access programs and Darkened [top secret] projects, as well as high level security systems attached to or having to do with submarine communications, tracking, and identifications."

McMoneagle concluded: "This is a down-range weather station and communications relay for Cape Canaveral co-located with probably a United States Naval Base, doing some sort of submarine communications relay, tracking, and identification. The location given the antenna field and stylization of buildings, vehicles, people, smells, air, layout, etc. would be Bahamas (80%), Turks and Caicos (50%), Virgin Islands (30%), and Leeward Islands (15%)."

The envelope was later returned to me with my seal still intact. For all McMoneagle knew, it could have contained a picture of my dog. Instead, it was an aerial photo of a secret Navy base, known as AUTEC, Atlantic Underwater Test and Evaluation Center, located on Andros Island in the Bahamas. The photo had been taken a month earlier by a pilot who had permission to fly over the base.

According to AUTEC's web site at the time, the base included an underwater submarine dock that is nearly the size of the base's land area. The web site stated "that AUTEC's vision is to be the Department of Defense and Navy range of choice for conducting undersea warfare testing and measurement in the Atlantic."

Even if McMoneagle had been given the photo, it's doubtful that his logical mind could have described anything more than a set of buildings near a large body of water with several helicopters visible. His description of the secret Navy base was uncanny.

Remote Viewing #1

Most of us will never come anywhere near McMoneagle's abilities to remote view, but the next couple of exercises provide opportunities to test your abilities. The first one is derived from the laboratory testing program that was used at the Stanford Research Institute, and is a good one for your first attempt at remote viewing. You need at least one friend, but two are preferable—one to hide the object and one to interview you. If you have only one helper, eliminate the interviewer.

While you are relaxing and clearing your mind, your assistant will place an object in a box, bag, or envelope and leave it in another room. Your mission is to describe the object, then attempt to identify it. The best objects are things that have several sensory details. A piece of sandpaper, for instance, would have color, texture and sound associated with it. A tomato would have scent, texture, color and shape. Your friend should stay with the object so as not to give you any clues to its identity.

After relaxing and moving into your meditative state, take about ten minutes to gather your impressions, writing them down or drawing a picture of the perceived object. If you don't get any inklings about the object after a couple of minutes, here are a couple of methods you might try.

- Tell yourself to move into the future and see the object in the palm of your hand after your friend has given it to you.
- Alternately, look into the past before the object was placed in a bag or other container. Use all of your senses: see it, feel it, smell it, taste it. Don't try to guess what it is. Let your sensory impressions accumulate.

Meanwhile, if a second friend is on hand to interview you, he or she should ask questions that guide you in new ways of experiencing the object. For example, if you are describing a round, red object, the interviewer might ask you to describe its texture. Is it smooth or hard? You might also be asked to look at the object from a different angle. Make sure that the interviewer doesn't know the identity of the object. You don't want leading questions that will taint the results.

When you feel you've gotten as much as you can, end the session by asking to see the object. Hold it in your hands. Feel and sense all of its qualities. Make a mental note of which characteristics came through clearly and which ones were muted or missing altogether. Notice whether you got sidetracked by the tendency to overanalyze. Don't skip this final step. It's important feedback in the process of learning the skill of remote viewing.

Remote Viewing #2

This exercise was also derived from the work at the Stanford Research Institute. It's similar to the first one, except this time you're going to attempt to describe a location. You'll begin your remote viewing at the same time that your helper arrives at the location.

Ask a friend to go to a specific place of his or her choice. Make sure that it's not an obvious place, such as a national monument located nearby or a coffee shop where the two of you meet regularly. Your friend should arrive at a specific time and spend about fifteen minutes there. She should look around, focusing on tall things or angular objects, soft and sharp things. Your friend should be aware of sounds, smells, and movement. She should look, but avoid making any effort to send you any information.

At the appointed time, you should relax and quiet your mind, preferably in your usual place for meditation. Don't forget to take several deep breaths. Then, as the time frame begins, jot down your impressions as they come to you. You might want to have another friend, who doesn't know where the helper has gone, ask you questions. Describe all the qualities that you sense, the shapes and sizes, the colors and textures, the scents and movement.

Examine the site from several angles. Try to hover above it. Look, but don't analyze. If you want, sketch the scene as well as describing it in writing.

When the time is up, your friend should call or text you with the location and a description. Visit the place as soon as you can and look for things that resemble the images you saw.

Don't be surprised if you get information that is totally irrelevant. That's just your mind's chatter getting in the way or your attempt to analyze rather than see. With practice, you'll be able to separate the good information from the rest. If you take turns being the viewer with your friends, you'll soon see how others tend to analyze and how that process distorts the original impression.

Mind-Over-Matter

Psycho-kinesis (PK) is probably the most dramatic and wondrous of all siddhis or psychic abilities—the power to use your mind to move objects, bend metal, even levitate objects and create an immunity to fire.

The first mind-over-matter experiments go back to the 1930s when a young man walked into the Duke University parapsychology laboratory and told J.B. Rhine that he could influence the fall of dice by the power of his mind. That led to experiments involving dice in which the subject would be told to toss the dice and try to get a particular number to appear. Over the years, many other investigators also attempted the same experiments.

Dean Radin compiled the results of more than one hundred experiments by more than fifty investigators over more than fifty years. He used every experiment he could locate so he wouldn't be accused by skeptics of only selecting the 'good' ones. The results showed that a genuine mind-matter effect existed, with odds against chance totaling more than a billion to one.

Meanwhile, at Princeton University, Dr. Robert G. Jahn spent 25 years gathering an enormous database on psycho-kinesis that clearly suggests the phenomena is very much a reality. He founded the Princeton Engineering Anomalies Research (PEAR), a group that conducted countless experiments under controlled, scientific conditions to measure the power of the human mind to affect matter.

Rather than subjects tossing dice, Jahn worked with machines, such as random number generators. For example, participants were asked to mentally influence the machine so that heads turned up more than tails, or vice versa. While the process wasn't as impressive as mentally moving visible objects, it's significant from a scientific point of view when a subject successfully alters the odds of the random numbers produced by the machines. That's because the process is fully automated, there is no way that a subject can contaminate the results.

A Moving Story

Nina Kulagina, a Russian housewife who grew up in Leningrad during World War II, developed astonishing abilities that were witnessed by scientists. She would sit at a table and stare at a small object, such as a matchbox or a wine glass, and make it move without touching it. She told investigators that she cleared her mind in order to concentrate on moving her target. When her concentration was successful, she felt a sharp pain in her spine, and her eyesight blurred.

One of the first scientists to take an interest in her, biologist Edward Naumov, scattered a box of matches on a bench where he first tested her. Kulagina held her hands over them and began shaking as if straining to force the matchsticks to move. Suddenly, all the matches moved together to the edge of the bench, then fell one after another to the floor.

Stories of this amazing woman began to reach the West through the international wire services in the spring of 1968. Two years later, an investigator named William A McGary described a session in which Kulagina caused several small objects, including a wedding ring and the top of a condiment bottle to move across a dining-room table. She also caused the wedding ring to rotate on an invisible axis on the table.

To make sure that Kulagina wasn't using a concealed magnet or threads, McGary often placed objects under glass containers, and nonmetallic objects were used. Films were also made of the experiments—some now available on YouTube—which confirm that no known force could explain the movements.

You might not be able to reproduce what PK stars like Nina Kulagina could do, but there are simple exercises, like the two that follow, that you can try. Remember to take time to enter a meditative state before you begin.

Flame PK

Place a lighted candle in front of you. Close off any air currents coming from fans or vents and sit far enough away from the candle so that your breath won't cause the flame to flicker. Make sure the candle is burning directly upright. Sit quietly, stare at the flame, take a few deep breaths, relax. Clear your mind of any distracting thoughts.

Now, visualize the flame shooting directly out to the side. Focus your energy on the flame until it bends to your will. Keep in mind that focusing doesn't require straining. Tension in your body might actually block you from releasing your energy.

Water PK

Pour water into a shallow bowl until it's about two-thirds full. Place the bowl on a table and sit facing it. Focus your attention on the water as you relax. Let your mind be calm and clear. After a few minutes, visualize the water swirling in the bowl. See it swirling faster and faster. Create this image in your mind. See it happen.

Then, the important final step: Let go of the thought. As you release the image, you might get the results you were seeking.

Next, we'll move from the siddhis to meditation and the power of healing.

Meditation Joke #4

Students achieving Oneness will move on to Twoness.
—Woody Allen

CHAPTER 12

Ease & Disease

"Our fear is not of the unknown, but of letting go of the known. It is only when the mind allows the known to fade away that there is complete freedom from the known, and only then is it possible for the new impulse to come into being."

—J. Krishnamurti, *The Collected Works, Vol. X*

When Tibetan Lama Phakyab Rinpoche arrived in the United States in 2003, the 37-year-old refugee was afflicted with diabetes and Pott's Disease. His condition was so bad that his right foot and leg had developed gangrene. He was examined by three doctors, all of whom recommended amputation. Rinpoche refused.

In 1986, Joe Dispenza was a 23-year-old chiropractor when he was struck by an SUV while competing in the biking portion of a triathlon in Palm Springs. He was catapulted, slammed against the road, then dragged by the vehicle after he grabbed onto the bumper to avoid being run over. He broke six vertebrae ranging from his shoulder blades to his kidneys. Shattered fragments of his vertebrae were pushed onto his spinal cord.

The orthopedic surgeon told him that in order to contain the bone fragments he needed surgery to implant a Harrington rod. This would entail cutting out the back parts of the vertebrae from two to three segments above and below the fractures and clamping two 12-inch stainless steel rods along both sides of his spinal column. If he didn't have the surgery, paralysis seemed certain. Two other orthopedic surgeons concurred with the first surgeon. Dispenza refused.

Few people would go against such medical advice. Dispenza was told by one surgeon that no one in America in his condition had ever rejected surgery. Rinpoche was told there was no cure for gangrene as advanced as his case—except amputation—and he might die if he tried to keep his leg. He turned to his mentor, the Dalai Lama, for advice.

The Dalai Lama's response was: *Do not amputate*. Instead, the Tibetan spiritual leader advised Rinpoche to utilize his skills with Tsa Lung meditation—heal himself, and then teach others the value of the ancient tradition. He also prescribed additional mantras, including *Hayagriva*, which is said to clear obstacles at the beginning of new endeavors and provide protection.

Both men healed themselves through meditation and visualization.

For Rinpoche, it was a decision that would require firm dedication to his beliefs. But he says he never had any doubts. "As a Buddhist, what is the worst thing that could happen if I die? I would be reborn again. But to lose a leg in one lifetime because I didn't try to save it didn't make sense."

So he began to meditate. Rinpoche says he took no medicine and didn't change his diet. He meditated day and night, only taking breaks to eat. In the early going, a putrid black liquid oozed from his leg. A few months later, it turned cloudy and bruising appeared. The swelling increased and so did the pain. The odor was sickening. Yet, he continued.

After nine months, the liquid running from his leg turned clear. The swelling subsided and soon he could put weight on his leg. At ten months, he was walking again with the help of crutches and before a year had passed he was healed and walking normally.

Rinpoche visualized *prana*, the universal life force or energy that is often associated with the breath, in yoga philosophy. Yoga breathing exercises are referred to as *pranayama*, the extending or drawing out of the life force. Rinpoche referred to prana as a 'wind' that is one with the mind. He saw it moving down the central channel of his energetic body, clearing blockages and impurities before moving on to ever-smaller channels.

Rinpoche had been a monk since the age of 13 so his belief was firm and he was an experienced meditator. Dispenza, on the other hand, wasn't an experienced meditator. At 23, he was an athlete with a new chiropractic business. But in the aftermath of his accident, his body was battered. He couldn't stand or even sit. He was forced to lie face down.

But Dispenza held a strong belief in a spiritual awareness that guided him. "I believe that there's an intelligence, an invisible consciousness, within each of us that's the giver of life. It supports, maintains, protects, and heals us every moment."

After refusing surgery, he was sent home where he began meditating for two hours twice a day — in the morning and in the evening. "I went within and began creating a picture of my intended result: a totally healed spine," Dispenza wrote in his book, *You Are the Placebo*.

"First, every day I would put all of my conscious attention on this intelligence within me and give it a plan, a template, a vision, with very specific orders, and then I would surrender my healing to this greater mind that has unlimited power, allowing it to do the healing."

But he knew he had to imagine the future he wanted. He visualized the way it would be, and became emotionally excited about it. "And as I selected that intentional future and married it with the elevated emotion of what it would be like to be there in that future, in the present moment my body began to believe it was actually *in* that future experience. " And his spine began to heal.

It wasn't easy, though. Over and over he would get caught up in his worries, thinking about what he *didn't* want, rather than what he wanted. Then he would have to start at the beginning again, mentally reconstructing his vertebrae, and re-creating step-by-step what he wanted. After six weeks, he was finally able to let go of the obsessing and analyzing. He found silence and he just didn't care any more about all those concerns and worries that had intruded on his meditation.

Astonishingly, Dispenza started walking again nine and a half weeks after his accident. He'd avoided surgery and didn't even have a body cast. The next week he started seeing patients again and by the twelfth week, he returned to training and lifting weights. "I can honestly say that I've hardly ever had back pain since," he wrote.

Science and Meditative Healing

Dispenza and Rinpoche have attracted the attention of scientists curious about self-healing by meditation. Researchers found that Rinpoche's brain changed dramatically during his meditations. New York University neuroscientist Zoran Josipovic, who studied the lama's brain, noted in an interview published with the *Daily Beast* that other studies of meditators support his findings. "What these studies have shown is that it is possible to optimize one's life experience through cultivation of subtle cognitive states generated through meditation, and that these are accompanied by changes in the anatomical structure of the brain, or neuroplasticity."

Scientists studying neuroplasticity have found that very few of our genes are static. In fact, seventy-five to eighty-five percent of genes are turned off and on by signals from our environment, and that includes our thoughts, beliefs and emotions.

In the thirty years since his dramatic recovery, Joe Dispenza has conducted numerous workshops and written several books about the power of the mind. He has also actively engaged scientists in his work, allowing them to study the brain waves and cardio-vascular changes of meditators during his workshops. In one such four-day workshop, a man with Parkinson's disease stopped trembling, another participant with traumatic brain injury completely recovered. Several people with tumors were healed, and others with arthritis experienced relief from pain for the first time in years.

Neuro-what?

Usually in my classes, the students remain quiet once I ring my bell and introduce the first meditation. But one day a few years ago, as I began a guided visualization, I mentioned the healing aspects of meditation and one of the students piped up, "Oh, cool. I'm into neuroplasticity."

At the time, I was only vaguely familiar with the term. I knew it had something to do with the mind affecting the neural pathways, but realized I should find out more. I soon discovered that a new generation of neurological researchers had coined the term: *self-directed neuroplasticity (SDN)*. Dawson Church, author of *The Genie in Your Genes,* writes: "The idea behind the term is that we direct the formation of new neural pathways and the destruction of old ones through the quality of the experiences we cultivate." Essentially, we need to change our beliefs about ourselves, and that can be done by connecting with our true selves through meditation.

My Story

I hesitated writing this chapter, left it to the very end. That might seem odd, since it's an important one, dealing with healing through the mind, through meditation, through our beliefs and emotions. The reason for my procrastination was not that I lacked information or stories about the inherent healing powers of the body and mind. Rather, it was because my own experience, it seemed, was a big failure.

I attempted to heal myself using meditation and other alternative methods, but ultimately opted for surgery. So how could I write a chapter that seemed to contradict my own experience? In fact, the night before I began this chapter I had a dream that reflected my concerns. In it, I was an FBI agent from the city of Z, and I was investigating someone who was also from Z and was making fraudulent claims. But when someone interviewed me about the case, the interviewer questioned my authenticity. "Are you really an FBI agent from Z?" That was when I woke up at 4:30 a.m., feeling quite relieved by the realization that I was not an FBI agent from Z.

I laid in bed in the darkness wondering about the meaning of the dream. By the time the sun came up, it was clear to me that the dream was about this chapter. I was about to write about our ability to heal ourselves, the incredible potential that our minds hold to repair and renew our bodies and change our lives. But I realized I couldn't ignore my own experience with self-healing. I would be a fraud if I didn't delve into it.

Let me start from the beginning. When I was in my late-forties, I began noticing that I had to get up during the night to urinate. Just once a night. But that was something new. It was also the beginning stages of benign prostatic hyperplasia (BPH), a common disorder for men over 50. It involves the formation of nodules in the prostate gland that gradually grow larger until they eventually press against the urethra, creating resistance for urine flowing from the bladder.

For years, I tried herbal remedies, such as saw palmetto capsules, that probably slowed the progression, but didn't stop it. I resisted seeing a urologist, because I didn't want the drugs that would be prescribed. I wanted to overcome this problem on my own without any side-effects.

As freelance writers, Trish and I were on our own. No company was providing us health insurance and we'd dropped our catastrophic coverage when the premiums kept rising. We were taking our chances, just as we did making our living as writers. We were healthy and instead of paying premiums, we opened IRAs and saved the money. The best bet, we figured, was to take care of ourselves and stay healthy. Besides, we were getting closer and closer to Medicare. Trish made it, and I almost did.

I did my best to ignore all the symptoms of BPH, the frequency, the urgency, the trickling flow. But six months shy of eligibility, my urinary tract completely closed down on Feb. 2, 2013, and I ended up in an emergency room. I left the hospital a few hours later with a catheter in place. At that point, I had no choice but to seek out a urologist. Drugs were prescribed, but surgery was recommended. I'd waited too long to avoid it, I was told.

At that point, I intensified my meditations, aiming to overcome this problem without surgery. Over the next several months, I continued to live with a catheter. I lived normally, still taught my yoga and meditation classes, still rode my mountain bike along rugged forest trails. Every few weeks, the catheter was removed, and I would go home hoping that my prostate had shrunk enough to relieve the pressure on the urethra. I would last a few hours, and end up back in the urologist's office, a walk-in clinic, or the ER.

I still refused surgery over the concerns of the urologist, who told me that the procedure was routine, and advancements in recent years had greatly increased the success rates. I would quickly return to a normal life. He did add, however, that my prostate was so enlarged that I might require a second surgery to finish the job.

I certainly didn't like hearing that. I continued to pursue alternatives. I meditated and visualized, went to an acupuncturist several times, had appointments with two psychic healers, and even underwent a healing session with a Q'ero Indian shaman, who was giving workshops in the South Florida.

Nothing worked. I was puzzled and frustrated. I would read the stories of people whose cancerous tumors disappeared, and other miraculous recoveries from diseases and disorders. People who had beat the odds and avoided surgery. Some of them had reached the point where modern medicine couldn't help them.

That summer as I continued looking for ways to heal myself, I heard troubling news. A psychic told Trish that her husband needed surgery and unless he changed his beliefs about what was possible, he would face a second surgery. When I heard that, I thought about my late father-in-law who had three prostate surgeries, and was never satisfied with the results. After that, I refocused my meditations, confirming over and over that, if I needed surgery, I would need only one.

In late August, almost seven months after my first trip to the ER, I scheduled the surgery. My Medicare had started three months earlier so it wouldn't be a financial burden. As I went into surgery, I was still affirming that all would go well.

And it did. Only one surgery was needed, and it worked. I haven't had a problem since.

But what happened? Why couldn't I heal myself? Looking back, I realize now that my beliefs were blocking me. Deep down I felt that I didn't deserve to be healed by some awesome means. I believed *that* was for people who couldn't get help any longer from Western medicine. I wasn't one of them. I was simply an experimenter. I just didn't have my emotions fully vested into the need to heal myself.

Emotions are Key

If you Google 'meditation and emotions,' you'll find numerous web sites, studies and general articles dealing with the quest to control your emotions. It's true that meditation is helpful in controlling negative emotions that disrupt your life. But you can also create or engender strong, positive emotions that help you achieve your goals.

Focusing on healing, Dispenza writes: "Many folks can intellectualize being better, but if they can't *emotionally* embrace the result, then they can't enter into the autonomic nervous system…

which is vital because that's the seat of the subconscious programming that's been calling all the shots." He goes on to say that studies have shown that people who experiences intense emotions tend to be more open to idea and also more suggestible.

However, in order to heal you must generate positive emotions rather than pessimistic ones. You need to avoid focusing on emotions such as fear, anger, hostility, and worry. Those emotions turn on the fight-or-flight mechanism, cause stress and impede healing. Such negative emotions block new information that can program your genes to change.

You don't heal, and you tend to repeat the past. As long as you see your life like the scenario in the movie *Groundhog Day*, doing the same things today as you did yesterday and the day before, interacting with the same people in the same way, what can you expect for tomorrow? More of same, right? That's especially true if you add a dose of negative thoughts to the mix. You're sending the same messages, based on your belief, to the same genes, and getting the same results.

Instead, by focusing on positive emotions—gratitude, joy, and appreciation—you open your heart to healing. Your body and unconscious mind accepts the emotional energy and reacts as if the healing you seek has already occurred.

However, you need to be convinced that you can change your present situation through your thoughts before you can generate those strong positive emotions that will bring the healing about. Let's take a closer look at that issue.

Analytical Mind

I've already mentioned my shortcomings at self-healing. Even though I was making a strong effort to reverse the condition, something wasn't working. In retrospect, I was trying too hard, trying to force the change. But I was also too focused on what I was experiencing and not focused enough on what I wanted. I was too analytical. I just couldn't get emotionally psyched about something that hadn't happened yet. From my perspective nothing was working. My prostate wasn't shrinking as I'd hoped.

I thought a lot about it. Too much. The more stressed I felt, the more I analyzed. I kept looking at my situation from the perspective of my current emotions, which relate to my recent past. So I was recreating the same emotions over and over again rather than the emotions I would feel when I was healed.

Some people naturally have more analytical minds. They're good at judging, examining and comparing, questioning and evaluating. Under stress, they shift into a mode of self-protection, guarding against dangers, ready for emergencies, wary of the unknown. People who are less analytical, on the other hand, tend to be more open-minded and trusting, willing to look at new possibilities, and explore the unknown. However, on the extreme side, they are gullible, willing to believe anything they're told without evaluating it. They make great subjects for hypnosis. (See the sidebar in this chapter about hypnosis for a really shocking story about how susceptible some people are to suggestion.)

There are times when an analytical mind works in your favor, and times when it actually works against your best interests. It's important to find a balance, and it's important to be able to calm you analytical side. An example of the latter is when you're pursuing self-healing. That's when you need to quiet the critic inside you, who is judging and obsessing, and open yourself to new possibilities. By doing so, you allow yourself to interact better with the subconscious mind, which enables you to move into a healing mode. You need to accept, believe, and let go of your doubts so you can connect with your deeper levels of consciousness, with your true self.

Probably the best way to quiet the analytical mind is through meditation. Here's a meditation aimed to do just that.

Shifting Your Mind

Start by settling down in your usual place of meditation, either sitting or lying down. Focus on your breath, taking several deep inhalations. As you relax, feel a rippling sensation from head to toes with each exhalation. You might imagine your breath like a stream of white light entering your nostrils, following the nasal passages and filling the lungs, then out again.

As you focus on your breath, let go of the outside world, your thoughts about yourself, and your analytical thinking about what you're doing now, what you did earlier, what you will do later.

Slow your breathing and imagine placing your do-to list and all of your concerns, issues, worries, and plans into a black metal container with a lock on it. Now see it slipping into the floor and out of sight, knowing that as you finish your meditation, you can take whatever you want from the box out into your day, and you can leave what you don't need or don't want.

Let go of your thinking brain and all of its connections with the outside world. Move your awareness to your subconscious, where you quiet your mind and become open to new possibilities, where the impossible becomes possible. Imagine and believe that the inner world that you reach through meditation is where you create reality with your intentions.

What is it you want to change about yourself, your health, your mental or physical well-being? Make note of what it is, but don't think about how you feel now. Instead, visualize yourself when whatever it is has been healed or is no longer a problem. How do you feel? How do you look? Infuse emotion into your visualization. Make it real. Adapt it as your reality. See it some more, feel it some more. Know that you are healed.

M-E-D-I-T-A-T-E

Hypnotic Trance

Meditation and self-hypnosis are very similar practices. But when an expert hypnotist guides a subject—one who is extremely susceptible—almost anything can happen, as this story reveals.

Imagine this set up: a master hypnotist searches for a truly susceptible person, one who would assassinate a VIP on command and then walk away without knowing what happened. In my novel *Romancing the Raven*, which takes place in the early 19th century and present day, Edgar Allan Poe has just been expelled from West Point when he is unknowingly enticed into a scheme aimed at turning him into a hypnotized assassin. His target: Andrew Jackson.

When I wrote the book, I was aware that the idea of a hypnotized killer was controversial. Sirhan Sirhan had said he was hypnotized to assassinate Robert Kennedy, but there was never any proof. So I was surprised to find out about a similar experiment that became an episode of a show called *Curiosity* on the Science Channel.

Called *Brainwashed*, the second season episode involved master hypnotist Tom Silver who started out with 185 participants in his search for one person who unknowingly would be turned into a killer and would 'assassinate' a foreign dignitary in a staged event. The participants were not told the true purpose of the show.

Silver screened the participants and found that 16 of the 185 were susceptible to hypnosis. He reduced that number to 11 when he weeded out those who might be psychologically damaged by the experiment. The remaining participants were divided into small groups and taken to busy restaurants for lunch.

They were hypnotized first and given the suggestion that their chairs would be extremely hot when they sat down and they would immediately strip to their underwear in the restaurant. All of the subjects complied to varying degrees, but seven of them were eliminated because Silver thought they were merely playing along or weren't suggestible enough to fully follow the suggestion.

The remaining four faced a tougher test, one that they could not fake. They were told to settle into a metal bathtub filled with 35-degree ice water. There was no way to fake this test. Under hypnosis, they were told the water would feel like a warm, comfortable bath. Each subject was monitored to test body temperature, heart and breath rate. Normally, someone exposed to water this cold begins gasping, shivering and their teeth chatter. Most people under hypnosis would typically snap out of their trance.

Three of the participants did just that. One lasted 18 seconds, the others just a few seconds. But the fourth subject, Ivan Santiago, a Philadelphia security guard, remained two minutes in the icy water. Even though Santiago's heart rate was high *before* the experiment, once he settled into the water, his heart rate slowed down, and he breathed normally. Santiago rested among ice cubes as if he were relaxing in a warm bathtub, which is exactly what he believed. His teeth never chattered and the instruments showed no signs of hypothermia. The researchers knew they'd found the ideal subject.

They then proceeded to thank Santiago for participating, and told him that he was being dismissed from the show, but asked that he come back for a final interview. The next day, during a break in that interview, Silver entered the room and instantly put Santiago under hypnosis with a tug on his arm, a pre-conditioned cue. Silver proceeded to tell him that a bad guy was downstairs. "He's got to be erased. We've got to get rid of him, and you're the one to do it."

He told Santiago that once he exited the building, he would see a red backpack on a motorcycle, and inside would be a gun. He told Santiago that he would grab the backpack and walk over to a velvet rope, where he would wait for a man, who would be carrying a briefcase. Then he told Santiago that as soon as the man came out the door, he was to shoot him in the chest. "But as soon as you do it, you'll simply, completely, totally forget that it ever happened."

Meanwhile, the scene was set. A stuntman playing the foreign dignitary was strapped with blood packs, and an Airsoft prop gun was placed inside a red backpack and laid on the seat of a parked motorcycle right outside the entrance of the building. A velvet rope line was set up and staged paparazzi were in place with their cameras. Two SUVs were parked on the street, looking ready to drive off with the VIP and his entourage.

So what happened? Santiago was a good guy, a trusted employee, a devoted son, a loving uncle. Not the type of person who would agree to kill somebody in cold blood. Would Silver succeed in turning him?

When Santiago walked out of the building, one of the producers shook his hand and said: "Ivan, you did a spectacular job." That was the trigger that was supposed to send Santiago back into a hypnotic trance. It worked. Immediately, Santiago looked around, saw the motorcycle, moved over to it, and picked up the red backpack. He walked over to the velvet rope line where the paparazzi were huddled, and slowly unzipped the bag.

Moments later, a man with a briefcase walked out the door. Santiago pulled out the gun and shot the man in the chest several times. The blood bags erupted, and the stuntman, posing as the dignitary, collapsed to the ground. Silver and a psychologist ushered Santiago away from the scene. Moments later, they told him what had happened. Amazingly, Santiago didn't remember a thing—until Silver suggested that he would.

It's a pretty scary scenario that someone's mind could be so manipulated. Now we know that it's actually possible to program a person to kill. Not just anyone, of course. But someone like Santiago, who is highly susceptible. That part of my novel has now been verified...and it *could* happen in real life.

On a more positive note, the experiment showed how the mind can affect the body to the extent that an ice bath felt like warm, comfortable water. Likewise, through deep meditation, the mind can heal and even journey to non-physical realities.

In the next chapter, you can explore another facet of meditation—contact with spirit beings. You'll have the opportunity to connect with power animals and spirit guides. It's all part of the world of shamanism.

PART THREE
JOURNEYS WITH THE JEWEL

Chapter 13

Shamanic Meditation

"In my opinion, it is unsafe not to know shamanism. Virtually all humans have unconscious connections with spirits, but the vast majority of Westerners lack conscious knowledge of them and thus fail to employ them to help and protect themselves."
—Michael Harner, Cave and Cosmos: Shamanic Encounters with Another Reality

Vision Quest

From my perch atop a large boulder, I gazed out over a branch of Canyon de Chelly on the Navajo Reservation. I hadn't moved for half an hour. In my vision, I was soaring over the canyon, aware of the presence of spirits. I was ecstatic, free of my body. After four days on a vision quest, I was launched on a shamanic journey, accompanied by spirit guides. Where would we go, what would I experience?

A distant voice cried out to me. I tried to ignore it, but the voice turned more urgent. It was pulling me back to the boulder. I heard it again as my awareness returned fully to my body. I looked over my shoulder. Of course, we were leaving and the others were waiting in the van at the rim. I'd undergone long days of hiking through the canyon, setting up camp, followed by shamanic rituals that carried on late into the night. The combination resulted in an array of mystical experiences that had lasting effects. I would go on to write four novels with Native American and shamanic themes, one of which won an Edgar Allan Poe award and another that was a finalist for the award. Meditation would become a regular part of my life, and as a meditation instructor, I would occasionally teach classes in shamanic meditations.

Shamanism has been called the world's oldest religion, dating back tens of thousands of years. It's not a religion in the traditional sense, because there is no faith or belief required. Rather, it's the oldest healing system, and was part of all indigenous cultures. It's about direct contact with spiritual realms, not only by the shaman, but also those seeking help and healing. The client or patient is an active participant, pursuing visions, possibly encountering other realities.

Typically, in Native American cultures, teenage boys would be sent on vision quests in which they would spend up to four days isolated in nature, often times without supplies. Their quest was to seek spiritual guidance and direction for their lives. During a vision or a 'Big Dream'— the term for a life-changing dream experience, they might encounter a guardian animal, a spirit guide, or a force of nature.

When I adapted the screenplay of *Indiana Jones and the Last Crusade* into a novel for LucasFilm and Ballantine Books, I included a flashback in which Indy recalls a vision quest he was sent on at age 18. Under the guidance of a Navajo elder, he climbed to the top of a mesa. Alone and without food or water, he managed to build a shelter and waited. The old Navajo had told him that he must wait for an animal to approach him and from that time on it would be his protector and spiritual guardian. Here's a brief excerpt.

Two days passed, and his stomach was empty, his throat dry. He wanted more than anything to climb down and find water. He stood up and walked to the edge of the mesa and stared down. What had possessed him to do something so crazy?

Indy was about to start his descent when he thought he heard the voice of the old Indian telling him to wait. Startled, he turned around. No one was there. His hunger and thirst were causing him to hear voices, he thought. But instead of climbing down the mesa, he headed back to the shelter.

He had taken no more than a dozen steps when suddenly an eagle swooped out of the sky, skimming low over the flat, rocky surface. The majestic creature landed on the wall of his shelter. He had found his protector.

Fortunately, you don't have to follow the path of Indiana Jones to get involved with shamanic meditation. This part of the book isn't intended as a course in shamanism. It's simply another approach to meditation with an emphasis on spirit contact and healing.

However, it's worthwhile to consider some of the basics of the practice.

The Essence

Shamans mediate between matter and spirit, between form and energy. Through their experiences, they become convinced that everything that exists in this world is alive and has a spirit, including the earth, trees, and rocks. According to shamans, we are spiritual beings manifested as humans. Our true home is elsewhere; our true essence is non-physical.

In addition, shamans say that these spiritual energies are all interconnected in a web of life. So anything that happens to one form of life affects the entire web. That's similar to Indra's net in Hindu mythology. It's said that one tug on the god Indra's net ripples throughout the Universe.

The most powerful shamans are master healers, and for the most part, are not happy campers. They've had traumatic experiences, life-threatening illnesses, or near-death experiences that have resulted in powerful visions, an initiation in which spiritual forces literally devour his or her body and mind, ego and emotions. Essentially, they become beings of light during their initiation and return to their bodies possessing magical powers and abilities. While most of us will not undergo such a shamanic initiation in our lives, we can participate in shamanic practices and meditations.

In spite of the influence of modern medicine and missionaries, shamanism has remained alive and even experienced a revival of sorts in the past several decades. It spread to the Western world mainly through anthropologists, who not only studied shamanism, but became shamans themselves. One reason for the popularity of shamanism is the easy access to the practice. Anyone can explore shamanic meditation. Workshops and vision quests allow those with a sincere interest to develop his or her own shamanic talents.

In part, shamanism is about honoring all forms of life, about healing, and keeping everything in balance. Shamanic meditations are usually referred to as journeys and often these journeys go into a higher world, a middle world, or a lower world. In these journeys, you might encounter animal spirits, which can play an important role in your meditation.

Power Animals

Shamans call upon animal spirits, which they consider powerful allies in their healing work. They might beckon a variety of animals depending on the circumstances, but usually they consider one particular type of animal their power animal. If you are drawn to a particular species—a dolphin, a jaguar, an eagle, whatever—then you might've already found your power animal.

If not, here's a meditation aimed at uncovering your animal.

When a power animal appears in a vision, you are encountering the archetype, soul or essence, of that animal, not an individual animal. The meaning associated with that animal should resonate with you. Think of the animal as a powerful ally, a guiding force.

Shamanic meditation is usually accompanied by repetitive drumming, rattles, or other percussion instruments that move you into a meditative/trance state. You can download shamanic drumming by searching that term or *shamanic journeys* on the Internet. It's best to listen to the rhythmic percussion through headphones or earbuds.

The Encounter

Settle into your place for meditation, either sitting or lying on your back. Turn on your shamanic beat, as described above. You might cover your eyes with a bandana or other eye cover.

Take a few deep breaths, and relax your body from head to toe. When you're ready, imagine that you're walking down a trail through a pristine setting in nature. Take a few moments to locate it. Maybe it's a place that you've visited.

Let the drumming move you deeper into a meditative state. Pay attention to each step you take. Is the ground soft and spongy or dry and rocky? Is the path gentle or rugged? After a time, you come to a large rock with an oval indention. It looks like the perfect place to sit down and rest.

As you do so, notice your surroundings. What time of day is it? Is the sun out or is overcast? Is it warm or cool? As you rest on your boulder, watch for any sign of animal life in your surroundings, either on the ground or in the trees. An animal might appear that seems curious about you. Greet the creature. Think of it as a new friend, your power animal. Ask the animal if it has a message for you.

Stay in this place and enjoy your surroundings until the drumming slows, calling you back. Give thanks to any beings that appeared, and any messages that were received. Retrace your steps along the path, and fully return to your ordinary awareness.

Animal Wisdom

If you've found your power animal, it's time to explore the meaning of the creature you encountered. Here's a brief guide to some prominent power animals and the wisdom they project. You can search for other animals in various totem guides, many of which are available on the Internet. Besides understanding the essence of your own power animal, you can use such guides to find the meaning of animals that you might encounter during your everyday life.

Bear

Bear medicine is about conserving energy, deep rest and rejuvenation. It's about exploration of a solitary nature. Bear suggests that you back off somewhat and let life come to you. Slow down, reorganize your plans and retire to your cave to meditate. Alternately, bear is telling you to stop hiding and get out into the world. You're well equipped to tackle the challenges.

Attributes
- Power and strength
- Solitude
- Rejuvenation
- Seeker of visions
- Individuality
- Recovery

Crow

Crow medicine is a gateway between light and dark, fear and hope. The crow informs that you have the freedom to choose. You sculpt your world as you see fit, confronting fear and overcoming it, or fleeing it only to face it again. Positive thinking allows you to solve problems in a creative ways. Clarity in your thoughts leads to self-empowerment and understanding.

Attributes
- Working without fear in darkness
- Moving through space and time
- Carrier of souls from darkness into light
- Moving freely through the void
- Guidance while working in shadow
- Honoring ancestors
- Understanding all things related to ethics

Dolphin

Dolphin medicine encourages you to live in the moment and relish it for all that it's worth. Allow the intuitive and spiritual dimensions of your life to shine through. Use your intuitive knowing to find your purpose and pursue it.

Attributes
- Balance and harmony
- Wisdom
- Knowledge of the sea
- Freedom
- Communication skills
- Trust

Dragonfly

Is she a dragon or a fly? She's a master of illusion and seems to shimmer in her iridescent body armor, echoing the shifting nature of reality. Dragonfly in its very essence suggests our world is a realm of dreams and illusion. Through dragonfly, you can see the truth in a matter. Dragonfly is a master of flight, hovering moving forward and back. She represents swiftness, change and elusiveness, and often acts as a messenger.

Attributes
- Understanding dreams
- Breaking down illusions
- Seeing the truth
- Swiftness and change
- Power of flight

Eagle

Eagle medicine tells you it's time to reconnect with your spiritual path. You can rise above any problems. You're able to place things in their proper perspective. Self-examination, looking within is in order. Eagle also teaches you to stay grounded, even when you are flying high.

Attributes
- Strength and courage
- Opportunities
- Wisdom
- Healing
- Visualizing spiritual realms
- Connecting to spirit guides
- Power and balance
- Seeing the big picture

Elephant

Elephant medicine is about dealing with your emotions. You feel things deeply. Family is important, especially the little ones and the older ones. You desire to serve others, but you need to nurture yourself as well. You remain loyal to others in spite of any difficulties that arise.

Attributes
- Strength and intelligence
- Connecting with ancient wisdom
- Confidence
- Removing obstacles
- Patience
- Royalty

Frog

Frog medicine recognizes the power of transformation. This spirit animal supports us in times of change. Frog is strongly associated with water and connects us with emotions and feminine energies. Frog medicine is about cleansing, physical or emotional healing, and also sensitivity toward one's environment.

Attributes
- Cleansing
- Renewal, rebirth
- Fertility, abundance
- Transformation, metamorphosis
- Life mysteries and ancient wisdom

Hawk

Hawk is a messenger from the spirit world. Hawk medicine allows you to see matters from a higher perspective, using the power of observation. You gain illumination, which allows you to solve your problems and to develop spiritual awareness.

Attributes
- Far-sighted
- Illumination
- Messenger from spirit
- Recalling past lives
- Creativity
- Truth-seeker
- Courage
- Overcoming problems

Horse

Horse medicine is about your inner strength and the driving force in your life. It's about personal power, passion and the desire for freedom. The energy is long-lasting, powerful. It's also about the ability to overcome obstacles and pursue your goals.

Attributes
- Strong emotions
- Passionate desires
- Physical strength
- Vitality
- Ability to succeed

Hummingbird

It's all about high energy and the lightness of being. Hummingbird medicine invites you to savor the sweetness of life. It lifts you from negativity and helps you express love more fully in your daily life. Swift and adaptable with its high velocity wing movements, the hummingbird can fly long distances, and can even fly backwards. Hummingbird teaches you to keep a playful and optimistic outlook and to find joy in everything you do.

Attributes
- Adaptable
- Resilient
- Optimistic
- Lightness of being
- Bringing joy into life
- Ability to respond quickly

Jaguar, mountain lion, cougar, Florida panther

The message of the big cats is about power. You have the ability to work independently or as a group, especially if you're in a leadership position. The big cat medicine allows you to embark on your own quest. You hold your own when confronted by others who disagree with you.

Attributes
- Gaining self-confidence
- Cunning
- Using power wisely and without ego
- Balancing power, intention, strength
- Freedom from guilt
- Empowering oneself
- Moving ahead in the dark without fear
- Seeing patterns within chaos
- Exploring unknown places
- Shape-shifting
- 'Seeing' distant events

Lion

A relentless fighter, the lion spirit represents courage and strength. Lion medicine is about overcoming difficulties. Lions also symbolize challenging emotions, such as anger or fear.

Attributes
- Courage
- Strength
- Group activities
- Personal power
- Animal magnetism

Owl

The message of the owl is about overcoming fears, maneuvering through the darkness, seeing what is hidden, listening to the cues around you. Owl medicine offers wisdom and skills that you need. You can access information that's hidden from others. Listen for news coming your way. Owl is also a messenger between the living and the dead.

Attributes
- Intuition
- Wisdom
- Exploring the unknown
- Inspiration and guidance
- Cutting through illusion
- Seeing through deceit

Snake

Snake medicine relates to an exploration of the mysteries of life. It deals with psychic energy and creative powers. It's about shedding the past and letting go of old patterns. Seeing a snake in a vision could also be a cue that you are ready for a deep shamanic journey, a journey of healing and renewal.

Attributes
- Healing energy
- Creative power
- Guidance on shamanic journeys
- Shedding old ways
- Letting go of the past
- Dealing with pain
- Exploring the unknown
- Life force, primal energy

Turtle and tortoise

Turtle medicine suggests slowing down, taking a break from your busy life, and getting grounded. Just as the turtle travels with its home, you want to feel comfortable wherever you go. Rather than bursts of energy in your spiritual search, the turtle suggests a grounded series of steps moving toward transformation. Tortoise is an ancient wisdom seeker and a treasure hunter.

Attributes
- Self-reliance
- Tenacity
- Patience
- Persistent
- Psychic protection
- Expert navigation
- Ancient knowledge

Whale

It's all about communication, often with distant sources. Whale medicine allows you to hear what is really being said. It's also about going deep within yourself to awaken your inner creativity. When the whale sleeps, one hemisphere of its brain remains awake, then it switches sides. The message is that you should pay attention to both the logical side and the intuitive side of your brain.

Attributes
- Creative
- Power
- Magic
- Nurturing
- Appreciation for beauty
- Emotional depth and clarity
- Well-being

Wolf

Wolves generally are group-oriented and hunt together in a pack. But a sense of independence is also part of wolf medicine. It's about establishing yourself in the community or group setting, working cooperatively, and teaching others what you know. It's also about leaving space for others to make their decisions, and not controlling others.

Attributes
- Teacher/guide
- Fearless confidence
- Working together while maintaining independence
- Communication
- Working in harmony
- Sharing knowledge in a structured way

Medicine Wheel

You probably learned in school that Native Americans never invented the wheel, a sign of a primitive culture. However, that's not exactly true. They invented a spiritual wheel long before Europeans were pulling carts with wooden wheels along rugged muddy roads.

While power animals provide guidance, the medicine wheel divides our world into four directions and applies specific meaning to each. It's a tool to help you realize your full potential. Medicine wheel meditations can reveal where you are in life and shows you areas that need work.

But I'm getting ahead of myself. Perhaps you've never heard of a medicine wheel and wonder if I'm talking about some sort of spinning wheel...or maybe the wheel of fortune. Not exactly. Even if you know something about medicine wheels, you might not realize that actually no one really knows what they are...or rather, what they were. By that, I'm referring to the original medicine wheels, the ones left behind from prehistoric times in the Americas.

Medicine Wheels were circles made with rocks by Native American peoples. Usually, there was a center point with spires of rocks extending out and dividing the circle into at least four slices. The Bighorn Medicine Wheel is eighty feet in diameter and estimated to be 300-800 years old. From above, it looks like a bicycle wheel with spokes.

While the rituals performed at these sacred places remains a mystery, it's thought that medicine wheels served as physical manifestations of spiritual energy, and were used by shamans in healing ceremonies. They might also have been used as astronomical devices for charting the movement of celestial bodies. Surely, the four cardinal points were honored as part of the narrative of existence.

While indigenous traditions have carried on medicine wheel healings, the meanings of the directions vary among the tribes. Some associate east with the rising sun, place of birth; south with protection; west with the setting sun, death and transformation; and North with wisdom of the ancestors. Animals also are often associated with each cardinal point.

Regardless of the differences, all medicine wheel rituals are about inner work as it relates to the outer world. The Q'ero, who live high in the Andes of Peru, have offered their medicine wheel interpretations to the outside world. Considered the last of the Incas, the Q'eros avoided assimilation after the conquest by moving their villages to high altitudes, and remained hidden for centuries. It was the Q'ero tradition that I was engaged in when I trekked through Canyon de Chelly, described at the outset of the chapter. We were guided by Alberto Villoldo, a medical anthropologist and Q'ero shaman.

Here's a meditation that involves the Q'ero method for pursuing personal growth through the Medicine Wheel.

Medicine Wheel Meditation

You might prepare for this meditation by building your own miniature medicine wheel, measuring two or three feet in diameter. I've done so in my classes. Once, I used origami objects someone sent me and other times I built a wheel with ripe mangos or avocados from trees in our backyard. Stones work just as well.

Whatever objects you use, create a circle with a cross within it, and align the cross with the cardinal points. Make it simple, so you can quickly build your medicine circle. Remain mindful as you create your wheel, then settle down for your meditation. Stay seated for at least a couple of minutes as you gaze at your creation. Think of your circle as sacred space, a ring of power. It will protect you and allow you to delve deeply within yourself. Think of each direction as possessed of power, each quadrant a house of energy.

You can remain seated, or after a couple of minutes you can settle onto your back. Take several long, slow deep breaths as you scan your body, relaxing each part from head to toe. When you're fully relaxed, you're ready to move on.

Begin by visualizing a circle of oak trees, and inside the circle is a medicine wheel made of white stones with crossing lines of stones marking the four directions. Imagine that you are seated in the center of this medicine wheel and surrounded by benevolent light beings or ancestors.

The South

In the Q'ero tradition, the journey begins in the South, which is considered the home of the Serpent. That's where you heal old wounds and traumas by learning to shed the past, like the Serpent sheds its skin. Understand that you can let go of emotional wounds and old personal stories.

If you have recurring memories of incidents in which you were hurt or offended and still feel anger rage, that's where you begin. You might immediately recognize the anger and toxic energy that you are carrying related to certain matters from the past.

Take at least fifteen minutes to allow one or more such memories to surface. If nothing occurs to you, don't force it. Don't look for troubling matters from the past. Let them surface on their own.

If your mind strays, imagine a snake meandering slowly past you. Or visualize it curled several times forming a spiral, turning inward, a symbol of wholeness, of the inward journey. You have no fear of the serpent, because it will do you no harm.

When a memory emerges, you can observe it without emotional reaction, as if it was from someone else's life. See each one and release it.

M-E-D-I-T-A-T-E

When you finish your meditation, know that those memories have lost their power to upset you. They are no longer holding you back from moving ahead. You might want to come back again and again to this meditation. Piece by piece all the heavy energy accumulated in your body will be released.

You'll know that you've completed your journey to the South when, in your daily life, you are reminded of an unpleasant incident and you don't react in the usual manner. You don't get angry, sad or depressed. You observe it without becoming emotionally involved. It's over. You don't forget old wounds and trauma, but it no longer has power over you. Whatever happened no longer affects you. You've freed yourself.

You can re-create your physical medicine wheel and enter your relaxed state whenever you meditate on one of the cardinal points of the wheel. You can also visualize the circle of oaks and the white stones that form a medicine wheel within the ring of trees.

The West

The journey moves to the West, where you encounter the Jaguar, who teaches you about life, death, and rebirth. Visualize the Jaguar. See its glowing eyes. Notice its power and agility.

The West is about moving ahead and embracing what's new, what's coming into your life. It's about moving beyond fear, anger, guilt, and shame. You learn to face fears and overcome them. You let go of relationships that no longer serve you. You cross a bridge from your old ways to your new life. Old, outmoded relationships fall away. You can now speak your truth without fear.

You move ahead with power, as a peaceful warrior. You no longer need to engage in battles within or outside of you. Instead, you are able to support yourself as you ask and receive what you desire so that you can leap into the person that you are becoming and journey into your creativity and your journey of love.

What is it that you desire that will take you forward into your new life? Focus on the Jaguar, it's glowing eyes, it's power, it's agility.

M-E-D-I-T-A-T-E

The North

In the North, you meet the Hummingbird and engage ancient wisdom and knowledge. We learn to manifest the impossible, and to receive help from ancestors. In doing so, we reconnect with nature.

You step outside of linear time. You can influence past events as well present and future ones as you become a co-creator of reality. You step inside the person you are becoming. You act with power and love. You release all the roles that you've identified with so that you have nothing left to defend. With your new knowledge you move through the world with freedom, flowing with ease, close to nature.

See Hummingbird hovering, its wings moving so swiftly they're almost invisible, it's body incandescent.

M-E-D-I-T-A-T-E

The East

Finally, in the East you encounter the archetype of the Eagle as you summon your destiny, and more. It's about the big picture. In essence, you dream the world into being. It's the way of the visionary who sees all the possibilities. It's about developing your vision of peace.

The Eagle guides you fully into the role and responsibility of co-creator. You take all that you have learned and bring it back into your everyday world. See the Eagle gliding overhead, soaring. Imagine that you are soaring with it.

M-E-D-I-T-A-T-E

Transforming yourself to the person you are becoming is non-linear and a continual process. You can explore any of the four winds, as the Q'eros refer to the cardinal points, at any time.

Today, in the Western world, medicine wheels are a holistic emblem that serve as psychological forums for balancing emotional, mental, physical and spiritual aspects of life. Rituals, mindfulness and meditation are the means for unlocking its mysteries. But you don't need to follow any particular formula. You can create your own personalized medicine wheel.

Here's a meditation for developing your connection with the four winds.

Finding Your Personal Medicine Wheel

Begin by preparing the same way you did for the other shamanic meditations. Each of the four directions should be separate journeys. Face the direction that you are pursuing. Maybe you light a candle or make an offering to honor the direction.

As you move from relaxation into your journey, pose questions: What is the significance of this direction for me? How will this energy help me on my path? Is there an animal associated with it?

What are the stories of this direction?

When the drumming slows, pulling you back from your journey, express gratitude for all that you received. In a notebook, or a computer word file called Medicine Wheel, write what you remember about whatever you were told about the direction. If your results were minimal, you might want to go back to the same direction on your next meditation. Alternately, go to another direction, and come back later to the earlier direction.

As you write in your journal, add any stories of your own about the direction. For example, if you took a trip to the South, what experience stands out in your mind?

Next, we explore journeys or deep meditations into the Lower, Middle and Upper Worlds.

The Journeys

In shamanism, meditations are referred to as journeys and the journeys take you into other worlds, known as the Lower, Middle and Upper Worlds. Such journeys provide us a bridge between our everyday world and the spirit world.

Of course these worlds don't exist in the same sense as our physical world. Shamans interpret them as 'places,' even though the spirit world is nowhere…and everywhere. That doesn't mean these 'other worlds' aren't real. In fact, all shamanic traditions around the world divide the spirit realm into Lower, Middle and Upper Worlds, and they say each world has many levels.

Besides, how real is our physical world? Its existence is based on our perception, our sight, hearing, touch, and other senses. We have a sense of physical reality, but there are endless interpretations of what we sense. Eastern traditions tell us that our physical reality is a collective illusion or dream.

The spirit worlds of shamanism are a source of healing, power, and information for those who explore these realms. The guides we encounter are protective spirits, there to assist us. They are not interested in directing, dominating or controlling us.

Traditional cultures designated these spirit worlds in the distance past, long before recorded history, long before Christianity. The Lower World is not hell and the Upper World is not heaven. The Lower World is a place where you can meet the archetypal or universal, mythical beings —the jester, the magician, the sage—and others spirits known through mythology. In a sense, the Lower World is a spiritual source for all of nature. On a journey to this realm, you might encounter prehistoric beasts, like the saber-toothed tiger, that no longer exist. Or, you might find a field of unicorns and winged horses.

Are you getting interested? Or do you find it too unbelievable? Maybe you want to gain more knowledge about these journeys. If so, I recommend books by the premier Western shaman and ethnologist, Michael Harner. His first book, *The Way of the Shaman*, is a great primer. His most recent one, *Cave and Cosmos: Shamanic Encounters with Another Reality*, includes some of the findings of Westerners who have explored the three worlds of shamanism over the past forty-plus years.

You can take shamanic workshops to learn more and partake in group journeys. Of course, you also can explore these other worlds on your own with the help of shamanic drumming. The best way to begin is to locate your entry point to shamanic worlds. There are many possibilities. Here is one method of entering the lower world.

The Lower World

Settle down into the place where you feel comfortable and won't be interrupted. Turn on your shamanic drumming. Wear your headphones or earbuds. Take your time moving into a relaxed state. Don't forget to take several deep breaths. Let the drumming take you into a trance-like state.

When you're ready, find a place in nature that appeals to you. Notice your surroundings. Find your way to a nearby stream and follow it. Keep walking until you realize that you're standing near the top of a waterfall that flows down into a pool. You can see the spray in the air forming a rainbow.

You notice flagstone steps going down along the edge of the waterfall and follow them. Now you see a path that goes behind the waterfall. You step inside the curtain of water and into a cavern. You see a tunnel ahead, and light coming from deep within the cavern. You walk toward it as the floor descends deeper and deeper into the earth.

You reach an opening and when you come out on the other side, you find yourself in another world, a place in nature with dramatic scenery, mountains and forest, lakes and rocks. It's as if you've entered a primordial version of Earth. It feels different from the world you left. The landscape is vibrant and filled with life. Your senses take in the richness of this world, and you start to see the beings who inhabit the Lower World.

There's a large boulder nearby and next to it is your guide. It could be a power animal or person, or a mythical character from ancient times. Approach the guide and greet the being. Pay attention to what happens on your journey. You might receive a verbal message, but it might also come through events and scenery. Notice if it's day or night, or if the sun is out or hidden. What's the weather like? Notice how you feel and how your guardian acts. Notice any smells or tastes. It's all part of the message.

M-E-D-I-T-A-T-E

When the drumming slows down, it brings you back into your everyday world. You might write about your experience in a journal. It will help you remember and assist you in future journeys.

The Upper World

I once talked to a young man who had been bitten by a coral snake and fell into a coma for a couple of days. When he recovered, he described a fantastic out-of-body experience that felt more real than this life. He visited a majestic crystal city—"an impossible city without foundations," he said. He called it the most awesome place that anyone could ever visit, and he wanted to tell everyone he met about it. The people looked human, he said," but they were more than human."

His experience sounded very similar to a journey to the Upper World. Fortunately, you don't have to get bit a poisonous snake to travel there.

You can access the Higher World in shamanic meditation through a similar process as you followed with the Lower World. Once you have relaxed and turned on your drumming accompaniment, imagine yourself in a pristine environment in nature. Maybe it's a mountainous forest or a tranquil beach at the edge of the ocean. See it, smell the air, feel a gentle breeze, notice the lighting. Is it morning, mid-day or evening?

This time, instead of burrowing into the earth, you will rise into the sky by climbing a rope or ladder, floating away in a hot air balloon, soaring away on the wings of a large bird, or leaping from a high cliff.

You continue rising and rising, higher and higher until you come to a region of fog. You pass through it, and on the other side you enter the Upper World. You might find yourself in a crystal city or a city of clouds. Spirits in human form reside in this higher realm and serve as teachers for explorers who make the journey. They answer questions and help us develop spiritual knowledge and wisdom.

Remember that the advice you receive is something you can accept or reject. Consider it closely, but make sure it feels right before you act on what you're been told.

When the drumming slows, you can return to your place of meditation by the same means as you ascended.

M-E-D-I-T-A-T-E

The Middle World

The Middle World is a hidden aspect of our world. It's a realm where the spirits of all living things exist and where these spirits develop the ability to shift into physical form. It's also a place where thoughts easily manifest into reality. It's here where our unconscious minds create our collective reality, which includes plenty of undesirable conditions that manifest into our world.

While the Middle World offers us the opportunity to create harmony in our lives and attract what we want, it's also a place where spirits of the dead cling to Earth, and where negative energy resides. In spite of these hazards, you can visit this realm safely to improve your life. But it's important to focus on all things that are positive, and not on anything that would cause harm.

The Middle World also is the home of ancient nature spirits, including fairies, elves, dwarves, gnomes, elves, mermaids and mermen, plant devas, and elemental nature spirits. These beings, which are considered mythical in our daily world, can assist you in bringing balance and harmony into your life.

An opportune time to explore the Middle World in meditation is when you are searching for a lost item or looking for information that can't be easily found in the everyday world of Google. The process of entering the Middle World is similar to the one you followed for finding your way into the Lower World. However, to avoid confusion it's a good idea to use a different means of entering the Earth. For example, if you entered the Lower World through a tunnel after opening a trapdoor hidden on the ground, you might reach the Middle World by descending through the hollow trunk of an ancient tree or diving into a deep pool of water.

You move into the Middle World where again you'll be met by a guide or guides who will show you what it is that you're seeking. When the drumming begins to slow, you return the same way you entered.

M-E-D-I-T-A-T-E

The work of shamans is a lot like what happens in deep meditation. Shamans enter altered states of conscious just as meditators do when they move past the internal dialogue, the concerns of the day, and turn to inner worlds. Shamans access the world of spirit, a journey that meditators also can pursue. I've heard stories from my meditation students about deceased loved ones appearing to them. They cherish these experiences, what shamans would call contacting the ancestors.

Shamans, both those from the West and those from traditional cultures, often express concern about environmental degradation and the future of the planet. It's also a concern of anyone who spends time in deep meditation. The question arises: how can we save humanity from self-annihilation, and create more harmony in the world? That's the question we explore in the final chapter.

PART FOUR
BEYOND THE JEWEL

Chapter 14

Meditation as Activism

"Be the change you want to see in the world.

— Mahatma Ghandi

Articles in magazines and newspapers tell us about scientific studies showing the value of meditation, how it can help you relax and become more in control of you life, and improve your health and well-being. That's true, and it's all good. But consider the idea of meditation as a tool for creating positive change in the world.

Those same scientists who found meditation helpful on a personal level, might be much more skeptical about using meditation to change the world. How, they might ask, can you sit around and meditate and change the world? After all, a drop of pure water falling in a mud hole doesn't create any noticeable change.

If you ask people what causes misery, the answers range from poverty, environmental degradation, and corporate greed to terrorism, big government and high taxes. All of those choices have one thing in common. What ails us comes from outside. During the protests in the late 60s against of the Vietnam War, the problem was 'the system.' And the protesters—including myself—were opposed to it.

It's not surprising that people who consider themselves activists say, *We can't just sit here. We've got to do something.* Such well-meaning calls to action can make us feel as if we're doing something worthwhile, something that hopefully will improve conditions detrimental to our well-being.

The problem is that no matter what we do and how hard we try to fix things that have gone wrong, we can't create harmony on the planet as long as we lack inner harmony. Shamanic teacher and author Sandra Ingerman notes: "...harmony within will create harmony without. Disharmony creates disease; harmony creates beauty and health."

It might sound as if *we*—the good guys—are part of the problem. The idea that spending more time 'being' and less time 'doing' seems to run counter to the idea of creating change. A humorist, considering the idea of meditation as a way of improving the world, might shrug and note that doing nothing might be better than trying to create change and making things worse. Meanwhile, a cynic might point out that the people who can change the world are wealthy and powerful, and they'll only change it to benefit themselves. Unfortunately, such sentiments tend to keep us in the muck.

The deeper I've looked into the question of changing the outer world and our individual roles in that effort, the more it becomes apparent that we need to balance action with inner work, that we can re-script the world by changing our own beliefs, by re-scripting ourselves.

In doing so, we are alchemists changing 'lead consciousness' to golden-light awareness. As we change consciousness and get in touch with that light within, we can instigate great changes. It's more about the person you are becoming, than what you do, that changes the world.

Renee Davis, who was one of the infamous Chicago 7 anti-war activists from the Vietnam War era, now heads the Foundation for a New Humanity and leads workshops in self-awareness. In an interview that's on the Internet, he said: "What I'm suggesting is that every time you blame, you turn your power over, and that the real understanding of blame on any level is a disempowering act—when in fact you're creating the whole thing....If there is fear as a dominant human reality, the fear is within ourselves. It's not an objective thing, it all comes from within."

In other words, everything that manifests on the physical level, first manifested in the unconscious or spiritual realm.

But how do we change ourselves, what do we do in our meditations and in our actions in the world? The first step is to recognize that we are not independent of our environment, of other people, of animals. We're all part of a web, all partaking in the journey of physical reality, all part of the same family of existence.

But look at the way we treat our environment and our fellow human beings, you might say. How can we sit and meditate these problems away?

Grand Unification Theory of Self-Empowerment

The answer is that resolving the big issues that haunt humanity starts with each of us. The real work is your inner development. As you meditate deeper and deeper, you attract fewer situations that give you difficulties, and when they occur you're better equipped to handle them. You see these problems that once might've seemed overwhelming as passing phenomena. You find more peace and happiness, and as more and more people pursue such goals, changes take place in your outer world.

These changes don't require everyone on the planet to become meditators. But a tipping point will be reached when what was only a dream becomes a new reality. Those who opposed the changes won't be condemned as we move beyond the 'us vs. them' mentality. There will be no victims, no losers, and no blame games in the new society that emerges.

Here's a chance to take part and get started. You don't have to be an advanced meditator to get involved. Your point of power is now, not when you're more experienced at meditation. Settle in, settle down. It's time.

The Inner and Outer Meditation

Create your mantra for changing the world, knowing that you are changing yourself, that's it's all about inner development, inner attunement. You're carving your inner path and manifesting higher consciousness in the outer world. You might focus on one of these phrases:

Inner peace/outer peace.
Inner harmony and outer harmony
Inner light/outer illumination

Re-scripting myself/re-scripting the world
Inner expansion/outer change

Once you've settled on your mantra, and moved into your place of meditation, breathe deeply and relax...relax...relax. Gradually shift to gentle breathing and spend a few minutes repeating your mantra. When your mind wanders, gently let go of your thoughts and return to your focus.

Leave more and more space between repetitions. When you're ready, imagine that you're in a place of nature walking along a trail that leads to a small rural community. You sense that there's a harmonious relationship here between humans, animals and the environment.

What is it about this place that's different from your world? Use your imagination as you visualize the possibilities. Don't limit yourself. Maybe you 'see' a world where important decisions are made through collective dreaming, where aggressive behavior is no longer rewarded, where cooperation has replaced conflict, where hostility, fear and suspicion no longer dominate the way of life. Maybe you ask someone what his or her life is like.

Watch for images or messages that come your way. Stay with it for several minutes or until you've learned all that you can for now. Come back from your journey and know that your meditations are helping create a new reality.

Changing the world also involves taking your meditative state out into the world. That's where a practice called *bodhichitta* comes in.

Bodhichitta

In Buddhist tradition, *bodhichitta* (pronounced *bodi-chita*) is about opening your heart. In fact, the Sanskrit word translates to 'awakened heart.' In essence, an open heart is about practicing compassion in all of our interactions.

Acting with an open heart possibly is the most important tool for creating a better world. After all, it's the way you would want others to act toward you. As more and more people practice mindfulness and focus on the meaning of an open heart, we move toward an enlightened society, one where cooperation is more valued than aggression or defensive posturing.

Here's a meditation for practicing *Bodhichitta*.

Creating your Mandala of Compassion

In this final meditation, we create a personal mandala—a symbol of harmony, wholeness, and unity. The mandala serves as a tool in our journey to heal ourselves and heal the world.

Move into your meditative state as in the above exercise, relaxing and breathing. When you're ready, imagine yourself seated crossed legged floating in a blue sky and seated on a small fluffy white cloud. Picture yourself with an open heart, and a sense of compassion for all beings.

Now imagine a vertical circle surrounds you and on this circle are your friends and allies, all of those who support you and encourage you. On another circle, outside of the inner one, are blinking stars that represent opportunities for you to express your compassion and offer support to others. As your heart connects with these blinking stars, they brighten and drift out to a third circle representing the entire outside world, and each star creates positive change.

The circles surrounding you represent your mandala for changing the world.

You can close your meditation by repeating two phrases, one in English, one in Sanskrit, in the knowledge that as we shift from a closed heart to an open one, we heal ourselves and we heal the world.

May all beings be happy and free.
Om Mani Padme Hum.

ABOUT THE AUTHOR

When Rob MacGregor started college, he planned to study archaeology, but ended up majoring in journalism. Over the next dozen years, he worked as a reporter and editor, but never gave up his interest in ancient civilizations. Between jobs and on vacations he explored archaeological sites in Mexico, Central and South America, Europe and North Africa. Those experiences would later come in handy when he wrote six original Indiana Jones novels for LucasFilm and Bantam Books.

Rob turned to fulltime freelance writing after he met his wife, Trish (T.J.) MacGregor. They wrote magazine writing and scratched out a living while working on novels. Within a couple of years, both were published authors. After finishing his first novel, *Crystal Skull*, Rob adapted the script for *Indiana Jones and the Last Crusade* and went on to write half a dozen more Indy novels, all set in the 1920s.

Rob is also the author the Edgar Allan Poe Award-winning novel, *Prophecy Rock*. Its sequel, *Hawk Moon*, was a finalist for the Edgar Award in the young adult category. Other novels in the series include *Double Heart* and *Time Catcher*. He wrote *The Ghost Tribe*, a prequel novel for the TV series *Peter Benchley's Amazon*, and co-authored two novels with Billy Dee Williams. He also adapted the scripts of *The Phantom* and *SPAWN*.

Rob has published twenty novels and fifteen non-fiction books. His non-fiction self-help books focus on exploration of the far reaches of the mind and body. They include several books on dreams and dream interpretation, synchronicity and synchronicity, the sixth sense and yoga.

Rob and Trish also wrote astrology books together for ten years under the name Sidney Omarr. Their greatest creation is Megan, their daughter. In addition to writing, Rob has taught yoga since the early 1990s and he also leads meditation classes. Find out more about the author and his works at his website: http://www.robmacgregor.buzz

Curious about other Crossroad Press books?
Stop by our site:
http://store.crossroadpress.com
We offer quality writing
in digital, audio, and print formats.

Enter the code FIRSTBOOK
to get 20% off your first order from our store!
Stop by today!

www.ingramcontent.com/pod-product-compliance
Lightning Source LLC
LaVergne TN
LVHW022324080426
835508LV00013BA/1309